# WAITING FOR
# THE LAND

# WAITING FOR THE LAND

## The Story Line of the Pentateuch

ARIE C. LEDER

P&R PUBLISHING
P.O. BOX 817 • PHILLIPSBURG • NEW JERSEY 08865-0817

Printed in the United States of America

**Library of Congress Cataloging-in-Publication Data**

Leder, Arie C., 1946-
  Waiting for the land : the story line of the Pentateuch / Arie C. Leder.
      p. cm.
  Includes bibliographical references and indexes.
  ISBN 978-0-87552-196-1 (pbk.)
  1. Bible. O.T. Pentateuch--Criticism, interpretation, etc.  I. Title.
  BS1225.52.L43 2010
  222'.1066--dc22
                                        2010010822

To
Stanley D. Walters
1 Samuel 2:9a

# Contents

# Preface

This study reads the individual books of the Pentateuch as contributions to its overall theme: Waiting for the Land. The book argues this theme understanding that the narrative problem of the Pentateuch is humanity's exile from the presence of God, that this problem is fundamentally resolved at Sinai where God instructs Adam and Eve's descendants through Abraham to walk perfectly before him, and that thus instructed and indwelt by the divine presence, Israel moves toward the land fully prepared to enter it and enjoy life there according to divine instruction. Because the problem of exile from the presence of God is resolved at Sinai, and because Israel does not enter the land, the Pentateuch reminds its audience that life in the presence of God is primary, and that possession of the land is secondary. The end of Kings supports this when it describes Israel's exile from the land, for desecration of the temple, as banishment from God's presence.

Many are the contributors to this work; I mention only a few: José Severino Croatto, whose article "Una promesa aun no cumplida" ("A Promise Not Yet Fulfilled") on the shape of the Pentateuch was formative for my understanding of the structure of the Pentateuch; Samuel Terrien, whose *The Elusive Presence* convinced me of the crucial role of the divine presence; and David

J. A. Clines, whose *The Theme of the Pentateuch* contributed the notion of partial fulfillment and partial non-fulfillment.

I dedicate this study to Stanley D. Walters, *Doktorvater*, colleague, and friend. Stan was Professor of Hebrew Literature and Languages at Knox College, University of Toronto, a vocation he exercised with deep respect for and careful reading of the biblical text. He loves the book of Samuel as a scholar and preacher. His study of Scripture, he once said, compelled him to preach. A short month after I graduated in May 1992, Stan left Knox College to serve Rosedale Presbyterian Church in Toronto as its minister. Knox's loss, the church's gain. He continues to preach and teach to this day. Thank you and blessings, Stan.

I am grateful to the Board of Trustees of Calvin Theological Seminary for providing generous sabbatical and publication leave opportunities, and to the staff of the Hekman Library. I also thank my colleagues who read chapters and made valuable suggestions. What you read is my responsibility. Finally, to my wife Olga, for her support and patience—it was always there when most needed—*¡muchas gracias!*

# Abbreviations

| | |
|---|---|
| AB | Anchor Bible |
| ANE | Ancient Near East |
| ANET | *Ancient Near Eastern Texts Relating to the Old Testament*, 3rd ed., ed. J. B. Pritchard (Princeton: Princeton University Press, 1969) |
| ANETSup | *Supplement to ANET* |
| AOAT | Alter Orient und Altes Testament |
| CBQ | *Catholic Biblical Quarterly* |
| CTJ | *Calvin Theological Journal* |
| CurTM | *Currents in Theology and Mission* |
| DH | Deuteronomistic History |
| EstBib | *Estudios Bíblicos* |
| JBL | *Journal of Biblical Literature* |
| JSOT | *Journal for the Study of the Old Testament* |
| JSOTSup | Supplement to *Journal for the Study of the Old Testament* |
| NICOT | New International Commentary on the Old Testament |
| NT | New Testament |
| OAC | Orientis Antiqui Collectio (Rome) |
| OBT | Overtures to Biblical Theology |
| OT | Old Testament |
| OTL | Old Testament Library |

| | |
|---|---|
| SBTh | Studies in Biblical Theology |
| *SEÅ* | *Svensk Exegtisk Årsbok* |
| *TDNT* | *Theological Dictionary of the New Testament,* ed. Gerhard Kittel and Gerhard Friedrich, trans. Geoffrey W. Bromiley (Grand Rapids: Eerdmans, 1964–76) |
| *TynBul* | *Tyndale Bulletin* |
| TOTC | Tyndale Old Testament Commentaries |
| *VT* | *Vetus Testamentum* |
| *ZAW* | *Zeitschrift für die alttestamentliche Wissenschaft* |

# 1

## The Story Line of
## the Pentateuch

Although the Pentateuch is not a novel like Jane Austen's *Pride and Prejudice*, it would be helpful to read it like a novel: a narrative that depicts a problem, places readers into a plot structure complicated by conflicts and cul de sacs, and that provides a resolution of the initial problem. Such a reading would disclose that the "old, old story" has a beginning, middle, and ending, that certain events happen before Sinai and others after Sinai, and that Israel never enters the Promised Land. This unsatisfying ending begs for a better solution. Joshua continues the story with great promise: Israel enters the Promised Land and receives its inheritance; but it ends badly in Kings: God exiles Israel from his presence. Thus the reader learns that the Genesis–Kings story begins and ends with exile and that this exile from God's presence is the reason for telling this old, old story.

Devotional literature and homiletical practices tend not to focus on the story line, but on smaller units, often without attention to context or connection to the story line, thereby encouraging a fragmentary reading of the biblical text. Knowledge of the story line is assumed.[1] But no one reads a novel this way, nor a letter from a loved one. A beloved novel is read through from cover to cover, time and again; similarly, love letters from one's youth or that hurried scribble from a battlefield casualty.

Should studies of the Pentateuch today assume audience knowledge of its contents? Do readers listen to the Pentateuch as a narrative with its own story line? By default, it seems, the pentateuchal story line has become unimportant to hearing the text. Even though contemporary readers are centuries beyond the Reformation's placing of Scripture in the hands of the faithful, might it be that, except for isolated cases, our knowledge of the content and the story line of the Pentateuch is not qualitatively better than that of those who received the Bible shortly after the Reformation?[2]

1. Since the Enlightenment the received story line itself has become problematic. Critical introductions to the Pentateuch have ignored the received story line and required readers to learn the similar, but still different, story lines of the Jahwist, Elohist, Priestly, and Deuteronomist writers. Commentary literature followed suit by placing sigla indicating these new story lines in the margins of the traditional text, or textual tools were developed to guide the reading of these new texts. See for example, J. Estlin Carpenter and G. Harford-Battersby, eds., *The Hexateuch according to the Revised Version, Arranged in its Constituent Documents by Members of the Society of Historical Theology, Oxford* (London: Longmans, Green Co.: 1900); S. R. Driver, *The Book of Exodus in the Revised Version with Introduction and Notes*, The Cambridge Bible for Schools and Colleges (Cambridge: The University Press, 1929). More recently, Anthony F. Campbell and Mark A. O'Brien, *Sources of the Pentateuch: Texts, Introductions, Annotations* (Minneapolis: Fortress, 1993). Recent literary readings of the Pentateuch focus on the received text's story line, but even these begin with commentary on and about the text. The story line is assumed or referred to with a brief outline. See, for example, Thomas W. Mann, *The Book of the Torah: The Narrative Integrity of the Pentateuch* (Atlanta: John Knox, 1988), and Terence E. Fretheim, *The Pentateuch* (Nashville: Abingdon, 1996). A notable exception is the story line of the Pentateuch in Joseph Blenkinsopp, *The Pentateuch: An Introduction to the First Five Books of the Bible* (New York: Doubleday, 1992), 31–33.

2. James D. Smart referred to this problem in the mainline churches. In his *The Strange Silence of the Bible in the Church: A Study in Hermeneutics* (Philadelphia:

Post-Reformation commentary literature recognized the importance of helping readers gain knowledge of the content by inserting an "argument," whether of the whole book or of the individual chapter, before the commentary proper.[3] By laying out clearly the major features of the story line in the "argument" and introducing the reader to its "scope" or central meaning, the commentator provided an outline of the content and a theological framework within which to hear the subsequent commentary.[4] Such reviews of the content and discussion of scope were clearly Christian: the saving of Noah's family indicates the reestablishing of the church; prophecies concerning the Messiah; Pentateuchal authorship by the Holy Spirit. The arguments in such commentaries point to Jesus Christ as the scope of the text; they provided a churchly, not an academic, reading of the Pentateuch.[5]

---

Westminster, 1970), 21, he writes: "the language and thought forms of Scripture as a whole are alien to them" (i.e., theological students).

3. As in Theodore Haak's translation of the *Statenvertaling*—the version of Scripture, with commentary, authorized by the Synod of Dort, 1618–19—*The Dutch Annotations upon the whole Bible, or, All the holy canonical scriptures of the Old and New Testament together with, and according to their own translation of all the test, as both one and the other were ordered and appointed by the Synod of Dort, 1618 and published by authority, 1637, now faithfully communicated to the use of Great Britain, in English: whereunto is prefixed an exact narrative touching the whole work, and this translation. 1657.* Henry Ainsworth (*Annotations on the Pentateuch and the Psalms* [Ligonier, PA.: Soli Deo Gloria Publications, 1991]) inserts a "sum" of the book before the commentary proper, and also provides a summary for each individual chapter. Similarly Matthew Henry, *Matthew Henry's Commentary on the Whole Bible, Vol. 1.: Genesis to Joshua* (New York: Fleming H. Revell, n.d.).

4. For a discussion of these matters, see Gerald T. Sheppard, "Between Reformation and Modern Commentary: The Perception of the Scope of Biblical Books," in William Perkins, *A Commentary on Galatians*, ed. Gerald T. Sheppard, Pilgrim Classic Commentaries (New York: The Pilgrim Press, 1989), xlviii–lxxvii.

5. This was not a novelty. Irenaeus, for example, retold the story of the Pentateuch in Christian terms, largely from a christological viewpoint. See Johannes Quasten and Joseph C. Plumpe, eds., *St. Irenaeus: Proof of Apostolic Preaching*, trans. J. P. Smith, Ancient Christian Writers 16 (New York: Newman, 1952), 54–67.

With the Enlightenment churchly readings began to be distinguished from academic readings of the text. Similarly, faith and belief from reason and science; each was assigned its own area of competence and authority. The distinction became an operational separation so that Scripture was studied and taught in universities separate from the church, or, in some church schools, as if they were not servants of the church. Objective scientific study of Scripture for the sake of recovering universally acceptable meanings was the goal and task of the academy; faith that of the church. Contemporary biblical research in its postmodern literary critical mode has moved beyond that position to where it denies the possibility of universal truth. There are no objectively right interpretations, only those legitimized by communities of interest, of which the church and the academy are only two. And who is to say these have greater authority than other interpretative communities, such as women's groups, or the poor indigenes of the Amazon basin, whether they belong to the church or not? David J. A. Clines writes:

> If there are no "right" interpretations, and no validity in interpretation beyond the assent of various interest groups, biblical interpreters have to give up the goal of determinate and universally acceptable interpretations, and devote themselves to producing interpretations they can sell—in whatever mode is called for by the communities they choose to serve.[6]

Such relativism is self-defeating. Why read Scripture at all, or any text for that matter, to seek instruction or wisdom? For some, as Clines argues, it is a matter of producing interpretations

6. David J. A. Clines, "A World Established on Water (Psalm 24): Reader-Response, Deconstruction and Bespoke Interpretation," in J. Cheryl Exum and David J. A. Clines, eds., *The New Literary Criticism and the Hebrew Bible* (Sheffield: Sheffield Academic Press, 1993), 87.

that will sell, whatever the market will bear for whatever interest group will buy. From that point of view the reader is privileged not Scripture, and it becomes the task of the commentary to help readers see themselves and their particular group interest values reflected in the text. Historically, however, the church has sought to help the reader hear the Lord and the values of the kingdom of God. For that reason the church has privileged the text and not the reader. With respect to the Old Testament the church has historically understood Christ as the scope of these Scriptures (Luke 24:27). From that point of view the task of the commentator is to enable the reader to acknowledge the scope of Scripture as addressed by the book under consideration. In this case that is the Pentateuch.

It is the aim of this chapter to describe the story line of the Pentateuch and to define its scope in the Old and New Testaments. I will do this by retelling the narrative twice: the first retelling will use the narrative's own vocabulary to establish the basic story line; the subsequent retellings will assume it and employ vocabulary typical of the church's reading of Scripture.

## The Story Line of the Pentateuch

Interpretation of any text begins with learning *what* it says, and *how* it says what it says. This is essentially an exegetical, not a hermeneutical, task.[7] An outline of the content can be useful, but it cannot re-present the genre. Reducing a narrative to the declarative propositions typical of an outline converts the text

7. See, for example, Jean Louis Ska, "*Our Fathers Have Told Us*": *Introduction to the Analysis of Hebrew Narratives* (Roma: Editrice Pontificio Istituto Biblico, 1990); and J. P. Fokkelman, *Reading Biblical Narrative: An Introductory Guide*, trans. Ineke Smit (Louisville: Westminster/John Knox, 1999).

into an alien literary phenomenon. It is possible, for example, to convert the Joseph account into a Pauline-like, dogmatic restatement of the doctrine of providence. But that would overlook the narrative character of the account and what Joseph's actions contribute to the meaning of the text. For that reason I will retell the narrative in story form, using its own verbs wherever possible. I will maintain the plot lines as they develop, are complicated by a variety of events, displayed by the principal characters in these events, and reach their *dénouement*. Instructional and other texts will be retold descriptively, with close attention to their own vocabulary, but as part of the narrative.[8]

> **[Genesis]** In the beginning God creates the heavens and the earth, and all creatures in them; he blesses them and commands the man and the woman to fill the earth. When Adam and Eve disobey God's instructions not to eat from the tree of the knowledge of good and evil, God expels them from the garden. Later, their firstborn Cain kills his brother Abel and becomes a wanderer upon the earth. Cain's descendants increase. When Seth is born to Adam, people begin to call on God's name. Adam and Seth's descendants increase on the earth. Noah's birth brings hope for rest among Seth's descendants. When people fill the earth with wickedness, God determines to destroy them, but he acknowledges the righteous Noah. God designs an ark for Noah and his family, along with many animals, clean and unclean. All these escape the worldwide flood and leave the ark when the ground dries up. Noah sacrifices burnt offerings to God, who promises never again to destroy the earth with a flood. God blesses Noah and his descendants, and makes a

8. James W. Watts, *Reading Law: The Rhetorical Shaping of the Pentateuch*, The Biblical Seminar 59 (Sheffield: Sheffield Academic Press, 1999), 29, writes: "Narrative invites, almost enforces a strategy of sequential reading, of starting at the beginning and reading the text in order to the end. The placement of law within narrative conforms (at least in part) the reading of law to the conventions of narrative."

covenant with him and all living creatures. Some time later God scatters Adam's descendants from the city and tower of Babel which they built.

After this, Terah, his son Abram, and Abram's barren wife Sarai move out of Ur of the Chaldeans. God speaks to Abram, telling him to leave his family behind and go to the land God will show him. God also promises to bless Abram with children and to bless the families of the earth through him. Abram and Sarai wait a long time for the promised heir; God eventually secures his promises to Abram with a covenant. Later, Abram promises God obedience with a covenant of circumcision. God renames him Abraham and his wife, Sarah. Abraham wanders through the Promised Land for 25 years before Isaac is born. Although Ishmael, the son of Hagar, Sarah's maid, is Abraham's firstborn, Isaac inherits the blessing. When Sarah dies, Abraham buries her in a cave in the field of Machpelah, which he buys from the Hittites. He then sends his servant to find Isaac a wife from among his own relatives in Paddan Aram. The servant returns with Laban's sister, Rebekah, whom Isaac marries. When Abraham dies, Ishmael and Isaac bury him in Machpelah.

Some time after Abraham's death Isaac prays the Lord to open Rebekah's womb, whereupon she gives birth to Esau and Jacob. Jacob, the younger, deceives Isaac to receive the blessing of the firstborn and flees to Paddan Aram to escape Esau. On the way, God appears to Jacob and promises to be with him. Jacob sets up a stone and calls the place Bethel. In Paddan Aram, Jacob's father-in-law, Laban, deceives Jacob by giving him his first-born daughter Leah in marriage, and not Jacob's choice, the younger Rachel. Laban requires Jacob to work an additional seven years before he may marry Rachel. Firstborn Leah is blessed with many children; Rachel has no children by Jacob, becomes jealous, and offers him Bilhah, her maid, to have children by her. Leah then offers Jacob her maid,

Zilpah. Jacob becomes the father of many children. Jacob also increases his flocks by astute management of Laban's herd. Laban becomes suspicious. The Lord tells Jacob to return to the land of Abraham and Isaac. Laban pursues Jacob. When Jacob satisfies Laban that he has stolen neither his herds nor family, they make a covenant and build a heap of stones as a witness. When Jacob nears the land, he discovers that Esau is on the way. That night Jacob struggles with God at Peniel. When Jacob meets Esau, he offers him a gift and Esau accepts it. After Esau leaves, Jacob moves to Shechem, where his sons Simeon and Levi eventually kill the Shechemites because of their treatment of Jacob's daughter Dinah. When Jacob arrives at Bethel, God blesses him. Rachel gives birth to Benjamin and dies. Isaac dies, and Jacob and Esau bury him.

Some time after Jacob returns to Bethel, his sons seek to kill their youngest brother, Joseph the dreamer. They sell him to traders who bring him to Egypt, but deceive Jacob into believing Joseph is dead. Judah commits adultery with his son's widow, Tamar. In Egypt Joseph becomes a steward over Potiphar's house. There God blesses him so that he prospers. But when Joseph rejects the advances of Potiphar's wife, she accuses him of wanting to sleep with her, and Potiphar throws him into prison. Joseph correctly interprets the dreams of Pharaoh's cup-bearer and baker, fellow prisoners. Two years later, when Pharaoh has troubling dreams, the cup-bearer remembers Joseph and tells Pharaoh of his wisdom. Joseph is released to interpret Pharaoh's dreams. After Joseph tells Pharaoh that Egypt will enjoy seven fruitful years and seven barren years, Pharaoh makes Joseph governor over Egypt and instructs him to prepare Egypt for the times of plenty and famine. When the famine strikes the whole world, it brings Joseph's brothers to Egypt and into Joseph's presence, though they do not recognize him. He accuses them of being spies but they deny it, telling him they have a younger brother at home and one who is no more. To test their truthfulness, Joseph requires Simeon to stay behind while the rest return to Canaan. When they return for more grain they must bring Benjamin, he says. When they find silver in their sacks of grain, the brothers become afraid. Jacob does not want them to return with Benjamin; he has already lost Joseph and Simeon. But when the food is almost gone, Jacob sends his sons, with Benjamin, back to Egypt. They return the silver and bring additional gifts. They appear before Joseph, who asks about their father. They eat with Joseph and then return, not knowing that Joseph has instructed his servants to put his own silver cup in Benjamin's sack. After the brothers leave, Joseph sends his steward after them. When the steward finds the cup in Benjamin's sack, the brothers are astounded and afraid for him, but they all return with Benjamin to Egypt. There Joseph tells them to return home and leave Benjamin, but Judah offers to take his place. The brothers explain that their old father cannot bear the grief of losing the youngest. Joseph then reveals himself to his brothers and explains that their selling him was God's way of sending Joseph ahead of them. He invites them to bring his aged father Jacob and the rest of the family to Egypt to escape the famine in Canaan. On the way to Egypt, God reveals himself to Jacob and promises that Egypt will be the place where his descendants will become a great nation. Jacob is joyfully reunited with his son Joseph. Afterward, Jacob blesses his children and dies. His sons bury him in the cave at Machpelah. Before Joseph dies, he tells his brothers that selling him to the traders was God's purpose, and asks that they take his remains to the Promised Land when God brings them out of Egypt.

[**Exodus**] Jacob arrives in Egypt with 70 descendants. After Joseph and his brothers die, Israel grows so much that they fill the land. Fearing Israel's enormous growth, a new Pharaoh enslaves them to build his cities, but Israel continues to grow. Pharaoh then instructs the midwives to murder all newborn males, but the midwives keep them alive. Then Pharaoh orders his people to throw every newborn boy into the Nile. Moses' mother places the newborn Moses in the Nile in a little ark; Pharaoh's daughter draws the baby out of the water, takes him home, and brings him up as her own. When he is older, Moses kills an Egyptian and flees from Pharaoh. God acknowledges Israel's oppression.

Some time later, God appears to Moses in a burning bush at Mt. Horeb and sends him to Pharaoh to demand that Israel be set free to serve the Lord. Moses pleads his own weakness and declares that Israel will not believe he is sent of God. God shows Moses signs and sends Aaron to speak for him before Pharaoh. After the first encounter, Pharaoh increases Israel's work. Moses and Aaron return to confront Pharaoh, but his stubbornness brings the Lord's terrible signs on Egypt: blood, frogs, gnats, flies, plague on livestock, boils, hail, locusts, and deep darkness. On Passover night, after God slays Egypt's firstborn, Pharaoh lets Israel go, but recants and pursues them into the sea. The Lord moves the waters to defeat Egypt, but allows Israel to pass through on dry ground. When the people of Israel see the dead Egyptians on the shore, they fear the Lord and trust Moses. Then Moses and Israel sing praise to the Lord for his triumph over Egypt.

After this Israel enters the desert, where she complains to Moses about bitter water at Marah. God shows Moses wood which sweetens the water. Later, when Israel complains about not having food, God miraculously supports them with manna; he also defends her from Amalek's attack. Jethro, the Midianite priest, visits the camp, praises God when he hears about Israel's escape, and helps Moses in the judicial administration of the people. The Lord brings Israel to Sinai, where, in his terrifying presence, he makes a covenant with her and Israel promises him loyalty. The Lord gives Israel many instructions and laws and prohibits Israel from serving other gods. Afterward God calls Moses to meet him at the top of Mt. Sinai.

At the top of Sinai, Moses receives instructions for Israel to collect offerings and to build a sanctuary for the Lord to dwell in their midst, and for the construction of the ark, other tabernacle furniture, the curtains, and other liturgical items. While God speaks to Moses, Israel organizes a corrupt worship of the Lord with a golden calf. Aaron helps in this. Thus provoked, the Lord determines to destroy Israel, but Moses intervenes. Although Israel deserves the Lord's punishment because of her stubbornness, Moses argues that God should forgive them for his own name's sake. Although many die at the Lord's hands, he promises to lead Israel to the Promised Land, and renews the covenant. After this, Israel voluntarily brings gold, silver, and other materials necessary for the tabernacle; she obediently manufactures the various elements of the tabernacle complex and brings them to Moses, who inspects Israel's work and blesses them. On the first day of the new year, Moses assembles and consecrates the tabernacle and the priesthood. Then the glory of the Lord fills the tabernacle; the fiery cloud would guide Israel on all her journeys.

[Leviticus] Then God calls Moses and speaks to him from the tabernacle at Mt. Sinai and gives him instructions for Israel's sacrifices: the burnt offering, the grain offering, the fellowship offering, the sin offering, and the guilt offering. The priests receive permission to take specified portions from the sacrifices for their sustenance. These are the instructions the Lord gives Moses on Mt. Sinai. The Lord instructs Moses in the ordination of Aaron and his sons to the priesthood. Moses ordains Aaron and his sons, and they begin their ministry before the Lord. When Aaron brings the burnt offering, fire from the presence of the Lord consumes the offering and the people shout with joy. When Nadab and Abihu bring an improper sacrifice, the fire of the Lord consumes them.

The Lord then instructs Moses and Aaron in the laws of cleanliness: the foods Israel could and could not eat; the priestly declarations of cleanliness and uncleanness for skin diseases, mold, and the emission of semen and menstrual blood. By keeping these instructions, Israel will be clean before the Lord. The Lord then instructs Moses in the matter of the Day of Atonement and the scapegoats, whose sacrifices would cover all of Israel's uncleanness in the Lord's presence.

The Lord requires all sacrifices to be brought to the entrance to the Tent of Meeting and he forbids the eating of blood. Then the Lord instructs Israel to live by his decrees, and lists prohibited sexual relationships. Israel may not do these detestable things, subject to being expelled from the land for defiling it. Israel must distinguish herself from the nations. There follow various laws and then more decrees about prohibited sexual relationships. Obedience will demonstrate that the Lord is Israel's God; disobedience will result in defilement of the land and Israel's expulsion. Israel must distinguish herself from the nations. There follow specific rules for the priests' holiness, unacceptable sacrifices, and the feasts. When the son of an Israelite mother and Egyptian father blaspheme the name of God, the Lord instructs Moses that such blasphemy deserves death by stoning. The Lord then instructs Moses from Mt. Sinai about Sabbath care of the land and the year of jubilee. Afterward the Lord teaches Israel that if they live by his decrees he will look with favor on the land, cities, and the home, and that he will set his face against them if they are hostile to him. These are the Lord's instructions from Mt. Sinai. Finally, the Lord instructs Israel to keep her vows. These are the commands the Lord gives Moses on Mt. Sinai.

**[Numbers]** In the Sinai desert Moses takes a census of all men ready for war, except for the Levites. The Levites are commanded to encamp around the tabernacle so that the wrath of the Lord will not come upon Israel. The Lord instructs Moses to tell Israel to organize the camp in military fashion: all the tribes in their places around the tabernacle, which is in the midst of the camp. In all its affairs Israel is taught to keep herself undefiled in the presence of God. Through Moses, the Lord instructs the people about keeping the special Nazirite vow, and Aaron is taught how to bless and place the Lord's name on his people. Then Israel follows the instructions concerning the dedication of the tabernacle. After the consecration of the Levites, the celebration of the Passover, and the appearance of the glory cloud, the army of the Lord begins its march.

The people complain about their hardships and the Lord hears it. Fire breaks out at the edge of the camp and people die. Israel complains about the lack of food and the Lord sends them an overabundance of quail; some die with mouths full of quail meat. Miriam and Aaron oppose Moses. The Lord explains Moses' special position. Miriam becomes leprous but is healed when Moses intercedes for her. When Israel arrives at the border of the land, Moses sends spies to explore Canaan; they report that the inhabitants are too strong. Against Caleb's advice the spies spread bad reports about the land. When Israel grumbles and muses that it would have been better to stay in Egypt, or better to die in the desert than to enter the land and fall by the sword, the Lord replies that they will all die in the desert—with the exception of Joshua and Caleb, the two spies who disagreed with the report—and that their children will enter the land. Those who spread a bad report about Canaan die. Against Moses' command another group goes into the land to conquer it, but they die. As Israel wanders about the desert, it receives instructions of holiness. The Levite Korah and others rebel against Moses and Aaron, accusing them of lording it over the people. The Lord determines that Korah and his followers will die for their rebellion. The earth swallows them. The Lord gives Moses and Aaron instructions for the priests' and Levites' service in his presence. He also instructs them in the preparation and use of the water of cleansing. At Kadesh, where Israel grumbles about the lack of water, Moses and Aaron sin at the rock that gave water. God tells them they will not enter the land for their disobedience. Edom denies Israel passage, Aaron dies, and Israel destroys the Canaanite king of Arad. Israel then complains about the manna and the Lord sends venomous snakes. Only those live who look at the bronze snake Moses elevates on a pole. After military victories against Sihon and Og, Israel arrives at the plains of Moab, opposite Jericho. There Balak, king of Moab, who is afraid of the multitudes of Israel, seeks to curse Israel using the seer Balaam. But God prohibits Balaam from cursing Israel; he allows him only to bless Israel. Later Israel herself is cursed for her sin with the Baal of Peor.

On the plains of Moab, Moses takes a census of the generation not counted in the desert of Sinai. The daughters of Zelophehad receive permission to receive the inheritance of their father, who died in the desert and has no sons; Joshua is appointed as Moses' successor; Israel receives instruction in the various feasts and in the keeping of vows. Israel takes vengeance on the Midianites and divides the spoils. Moses tells the Gadites and Reubenites, who are receiving their possession, not to repeat the rebellion of the first generation. After a list of the stages of Israel's journey and a description of the boundaries of Canaan, Israel receives instructions concerning the distribution of the land, the inheritance of the Levites, and the cities of refuge. Then the Lord commands Moses to allow Zelophehad's daughters to keep their inheritance if they do not marry outside of their tribe, for each tribe is to keep the land it inherits. These are the regulations the Lord gives Israel through Moses on the plains of Moab across from Jericho.

[**Deuteronomy**] In the fortieth year and the eleventh month of their wanderings, Moses tells Israel all that the Lord has commanded him. He is east of the Jordan, in Moab, when he gives Israel this instruction (*torah*): Beginning with their stay at Horeb, Moses tells Israel that at that time God told them to break camp to go to the land of the Amorites according to his promises to Abraham, Isaac, and Jacob, and that God appointed leaders to help Moses. Moses then reminds Israel of the spies, their rebellion against God, his punishment, the defeats Israel suffered, and their victories against Sihon and Og. He also reminds them that Reuben, Gad, and half the tribe of Manasseh inherited their possessions on the east side of the Jordan; and that God did not permit him, Moses, to enter the land, but did let him see it from Mt. Pisgah. He then urges Israel to hear the law (*torah*): How Israel suffered God's punishment at Baal of Peor, that God's decrees are Israel's wisdom among the nations, that when God spoke to them Israel saw no form, that Moses would die outside the land for his rebellion, that they ought to refrain from idolatry but know that besides the Lord there is no other. Moses then recites the covenant words to those who are alive (on the plains of Moab), reminds Israel to serve the Lord alone with all their heart, mind, and soul. Furthermore, he teaches Israel to observe the law so their children may inherit the land; that will be their righteousness. They should not serve the gods of Canaan nor allow their children to intermarry with the Canaanites. Doing so will bring God to withhold the rain from the land. When they get to the land filled with all good things they will remember the Lord and his care in the desert, and not forget him, or they will disappear among the nations. Moses reminds Israel that they are entering the land because of the wickedness of the nations, not her own righteousness. They should remember the golden calf and then how God did not destroy Israel. Israel should fear the Lord, and love and obey him alone.

When Israel possesses the land, she must worship the Lord at the place he chooses and worship no other gods. She must remember to eat foods declared to be clean, pay her tithes, cancel debts according to the law, and regularly celebrate all her feasts. Israel's king is to rule according to the law. The Lord will raise up a prophet for Israel, one like Moses. He teaches them to keep various and sundry laws when God gives them the land.

Moses then tells the people that when they get into the land they must gather on Mt. Ebal and pronounce the curses of the covenant. He also instructs them in the blessings that will come upon her if she obeys the Lord, and the curses if she disobeys.

These are the terms of the covenant the Lord makes with Israel through Moses, in Moab. Joshua will succeed Moses, the people are instructed to read this law (*torah*) every seven years. The Lord tells Moses that Israel will rebel when they get into the land, and Moses sings a song as God's witness against Israel. Moses prepares for his death. He pronounces a blessing on Israel, is allowed to see the land, and dies in Moab. Joshua receives the spirit of wisdom because Moses laid his hands on him. Since then there has not arisen a prophet in Israel like Moses, whom the Lord knew face to face.

## The Scope of the Pentateuch in the Old Testament

From the call of Abraham in Genesis through Deuteronomy, the Pentateuch narrates the story of Abraham, Isaac, and Jacob, and their descendants, none of whom enters the land to possess it. Although Abraham arrives in Canaan, he remains a total stranger to and in it; he has to buy property to bury his beloved Sarah. Abraham roots his life in God's promise of land, not in the land itself. The patriarchal family receives the surety of the promise only in their burial in the cave at Machpelah. When

16

Abraham's post-Egypt descendants reach the plains of Moab, they remain there. Like Abraham and his household, they are a pilgrim community who await the fullness of the promise of land. There, as they have since Egypt, Israel receives Moses' instructions. But he will not lead them into the land.

Moses is Israel's supreme catechist. With divine instruction, he sculpts Israel into the people God desires: one awaiting God's future in his gracious presence. From Sinai, Moses mediates the covenant between God and Israel, and discloses the design for the instrument of God's presence, the Tent of Meeting, from which God reveals his will for holy and clean living. When Israel does what Moses commands, they do God's will; when they rebel against him, they speak against the very voice of God (Num. 12). When they believe in him, having seen the mighty works of God (Ex. 14:31), they trust the one who is uniquely God's servant chosen to reveal God's will upon earth and bring his people out of bondage. When Israel does enter the land, Joshua reminds her to live there according to the "law my servant Moses gave you" (Josh. 1:7). If Israel lives according to Moses' law, she will fully enjoy the promises of God. Moses, the prophet than whom no greater arose in the Old Testament, is the scope of the Pentateuch (Deut. 34:10–12).

## A Christian Rereading of the Pentateuch

Anyone reading the Pentateuch wants to know why this ancient story is relevant for redeeming and shaping human life and conduct in the twenty-first century. Christians acknowledge the privileged role of the Old and New Testaments, that these texts have created and molded them as a people, and that they read them not as a *novum*, but as texts that have shaped their ancestors in the faith, texts that now also direct them as members of the same community. The Christian church, in all times and places, believes that these Scriptures are unique among all written texts, sacred and secular, because they reveal the will of God, without which no one can truly live in the presence of God. And since Jesus Christ is the fullness of this revelation, Christians cannot read any of the Scriptures without hearing him. For that reason Christians read the Pentateuch as part of the Christian canon.

When the church reads the Pentateuch in this way, it does not neglect the books' historical context, that is, that before Christ's coming these words were addressed to Abraham's descendants. For that reason, we defined the scope of the Pentateuch as Moses: in the Old Testament there was no one else who so clearly revealed God's will for his people. After God's self-disclosure in Christ, however, we read the Pentateuch as part of Christian Scripture, which testifies to what God has done through his people and is doing through Jesus Christ.

A Christian reading assumes that the biblical text belongs to and shapes an interpretative community, the church of Christ, and that the Christian interpreter does not stand objectively over against this community, nor as a representative of an interest that is alien to this interpretative community.[9] Thus the following synopsis of the *Dutch Annotations*, which uses vocabulary typical of the church, is recognizable by Christians everywhere.[10]

---

9. Reflecting Gadamer, A. D. H. Mayes writes, "The 'anticipation of meaning' or the preliminary projection of the sense of the text as a whole derives not simply from the interpreter but rather from the tradition to which both the text and interpreter belong." "On Describing the Purpose of Deuteronomy," *JSOT* 58 (1993): 20. Postmodern studies stay within this framework, but redefine the tradition to which the interpreter and the text belong as interest groups.

10. Haak, *The Dutch Annotations upon the Whole Bible*. I have left the original orthography.

In the beginning God created all things visible and invisible through his word, out of nothing. He made man in the image of God. Here we find the original rise of sin and death in Adam and Eve, the first promise of grace concerning man's redemption, and the rudiments of sound doctrine of the true religion, and of the worship of God. The history of the true church from Adam through Noah, and through Noah after the flood. Moses shows the re-establishment of the church, its preservation through Shem, and after Shem fell into idolatry out of grace God singled out Abraham that the Messiah should be born of his seed. God maintained this chosen generation by his word and Spirit, forgave the patriarchs' sin for the Messiah's sake, whom they embraced with true repentance. When they die, Joseph being the last, they leave behind excellent testimonies of their faith in God's promises. This history comprises more than 2300 years.

In Exodus the Holy Ghost shows the increase of Israel under Pharaoh's oppression and the wonderful birth and preservation of Moses. He shows how God with great plagues delivers his people by Moses after they had eaten the Paschal Lamb, guided and provided for them through the wilderness, where at Sinai they received the Ten Commandments and instructions for the tabernacle. Moses' intercession saves Israel from God's destruction for having built the golden calf. God renews the covenant, the people make offerings for the making of the tabernacle. After the tabernacle was assembled it was anointed and filled with God's glory. This history took place during some 142 years.

Leviticus contains God's ordinances for the maintenance of God's public and holy worship. These are for the most part ceremonial laws; to them are joined various moral laws and civil ordinances punishable by the magistrate. Narratives of the ordination of priests and the punishment of a blasphemer are also included. All this happened during one month.

Numbers tells of the organization of the camp through its journeys through the wilderness; it speaks of the offices of the priests and Levites, describes ceremonial, moral and civil laws, and describes events which yield many instructions and warnings for all men, for civil and ecclesiastical affairs. It tells of Israel's murmurings and their punishments. Moses receives the help of 70 "ancient men (or Senators)" to govern Israel, suffers opposition, and Israel's refusal to enter the land leads to their wandering until the 40th year after they leave Egypt. Numbers conceals neither Israel's sin and punishment nor the virtues and good works of godly and pious men together with their promised reward. Preeminent is Moses' intercessory prayer for the rebellious generation. God shows his spiritual favor by maintaining pure religion and worship, and temporal mercy in delivering them from their enemies. Last, Israel prepares itself for entry into the land. This book contains historical acts of 38 years and nine months.

In the two last months of the fortieth year Moses, knowing he will soon die and not enter Canaan, repeats the laws recorded in the foregoing books to instruct those who had grown up in the wilderness in their duty. First he recounts God's mercies over the forty years to prepare them for obedience to the commandments. Then he repeats the moral law of the ten commandments together with ceremonial, civil, and military ordinances, including some new laws, and a remarkable prophecy concerning Jesus Christ. He promises blessings upon obedience and curses upon those who depart from the law. He charges Israel to read the Book of the Law regularly and then teaches them a prophetic song foretelling what will happen to them until the coming of Christ and the calling of the Gentiles. Moses views the land, dies, and Joshua takes his place.

# The Scope of the Pentateuch
## as Christian Scripture

This churchly reading, clear to any seventeenth-century Christian, was not academically naive. An examination of exegetical works such as Henry Ainsworth's *Annotations on the Pentateuch and the Psalms* discloses that the authors were acutely aware of historical distance and linguistic, textual, and hermeneutical issues. Nevertheless, they do not treat the text as an historical antiquity, but as Christian Scripture, an ancient text that is theologically transparent to the readers of the *Dutch Annotations*. This is clear from the language typical of the Christian theological tradition: God created "all things visible and invisible," he did so "through his word, out of nothing," and he endowed man "with the image of God." Although ancient, these depicted historical events speak eternal truths to present realities: the church, its public worship and sound doctrine, temporal as well as eternal blessings, and punishment for behavior not consonant with God's law; above all, they point to the Messiah.

Central to this reading of the Pentateuch is the pure doctrine by which God shapes his people in worship and conduct, and the hope represented by Jesus Christ, the prophet greater than Moses, who discloses the fullness of God's will, and who mediates between God and the people awaiting the fullness of divine promises. Christ, who comes from the Father, shapes that waiting with his instructions. A Christian reading holds Christ to be the scope of the Pentateuch. This reading comports with the Pentateuch's scope: divine instruction for God's people, delivered centrally at Sinai in the Lord's presence, for the shaping of a people of his own selection. Even as the voice of the Lord through Moses is central to the Pentateuch, so the incarnate voice of God in Jesus Christ is central to the gospel (Matt. 17:5).

## Waiting for the Land

In the following chapters we will read the Pentateuch, paying attention to its story line and that of the individual books. We will note that Adam's descendants, exiled from God's presence, are aimless wanderers, that from among them God redirects Abram and Sarai, instructing them to go to the Promised Land, but that neither they nor their descendants enter the land in the Pentateuch. God does bring them into his presence at Sinai. This solves the fundamental problem of the exile from God and changes the shape of waiting for the fulfillment of the land promise, for they wait in the presence of God. At the conclusion of each of the books, we will briefly reflect how that book contributes to the theme of waiting for the land in God's presence. The final chapter will reflect on waiting for the land in God's presence today.

# 2

# The Plot, Scope, and Structure of the Pentateuch

Having reviewed the story line of the Pentateuch we now turn to examine its plot and structure with a view to understanding the shape and message of this narrative.

## Plot and the Biblical Narrative

In its simplest form, narrative has a beginning, middle, and end. It moves from beginning to end by means of emplotted events, complications, and conflicts, to a resolution of the initially defined narrative problem. Plot, reasons Fokkelman,

> determines the boundaries of the story as a meaningful whole. These boundaries . . . in their own way, draw the horizon of our correct understanding of the story: within it, the reader is looking for the connections between everything and everything else. . . . The full-grown story begins by establishing a problem

or deficit; next it can present an exposition before the action gets urgent; obstacles and conflicts may occur that attempt to frustrate the *dénouement,* and finally there is the winding up, which brings the solution of the problem or the cancellation of the deficit.[1]

Keeping this in mind, and looking at the entire biblical narrative, we note that Adam and Eve's refusal of divine instruction and consequent exile from the garden of Eden and God's presence, defines the narrative problem or deficit which initiates a series of events, complications, and conflicts between the Creator and humanity that come to a certain resolution with God's selection of Abraham and the promise of land, progeny, and blessing. This selection itself begins another series of events, complications, and conflicts which concludes with Israel's waiting to enter the Promised Land (Genesis–Deuteronomy). Continuing with the Former Prophets: Israel's entry into the land initiates yet another sequence of events, complications, and conflicts that concludes with the destruction of Jerusalem and Judah's exile (Joshua–Kings). Genesis–Kings begins and ends with an exile; at the end of Kings, Israel is waiting for the land, again. In her exile Israel suffers the same consequences that Adam and Eve did: expulsion from the presence of God (2 Kings 17:18, 20, 23; 23:27; 24:3, 20), not from the land. Life is not a matter of being rooted in a particular soil, but in the presence of God. Thus, the narrative problem defined at the beginning of Genesis has not been resolved, not at the end of Deuteronomy, nor at the end of Kings; it has merely been restated. Not even the narratives

---

1. J. P. Fokkelman, *Reading Biblical Narrative: An Introductory Guide,* trans. Ineke Smit (Louisville: Westminster/John Knox, 1999), 77. Conflict is crucial to the development of plot. Claus Westermann (*The Promises to the Fathers: Studies on the Patriarchal Narratives* [Philadelphia: Fortress, 1980], 36) writes that "a narrative gives literary form to a sequence of events leading from tension to its resolution."

addressed to the post-exilic community, Ezra–Nehemiah, declare a resolution; only a repetition of the old problems: intermarriage, Sabbath breaking, and defilement of the temple (Neh. 13). Not even a return to the land solves the problem of Israel's exile from the presence of God. Post-exilic Israel continues her waiting, but now with the burden of a shameful and sorrowful memory of one constant: her defilement of God's presence.

A Christian reading of the Old Testament narrative understands that Jesus Christ's coming solves the problem of Israel's exile from the presence of God, for he is "God with us" (Matt. 1:16, 23; 28:20b; John 1:14). But Christ's ascension complicates the narrative again; he is no longer with us as he was during his earthly ministry. And even though his Spirit indwells the body of Christ, the ecclesial community experiences much conflict (John 16:33) as it awaits the anticipated resolution and the promised rest in the land (1 Thess. 4:13–18; Heb. 4; Rev. 21) in the new creation (2 Peter 3:13). Exile from the presence of God, then, forms the boundaries of the entire biblical narrative, as well as of its various subunits (i.e., Genesis–Kings).

The entire biblical narrative, then, develops the problem of humanity's refusal of divine instruction and exile from the presence of God and emplots a sequence of events, complications, and conflicts that brings about life in God's presence again. Within this larger narrative, the Pentateuch develops a plot that depicts a particular community, Abraham's descendants, on the way to the Promised Land, the place the Lord chose to dwell (i.e., the presence of God), but they do not enter the land. At the end of the Pentateuch, Israel is on the plains of Moab, opposite Jericho, waiting to enter the land. And because the land is the place where God will dwell among his people, Israel's waiting on the plains of Moab is not unlike her descendants waiting by the rivers of Babel: at the end of the Pentateuch Israel is in "exile." And because it ends this way, the Pentateuch brings every generation of God's people who reads it back to the plains of Moab, where it waits to enter the land.[2]

## The Narrative Problem of the Pentateuch: Refusal of Divine Instruction and Exile

Although from Genesis 11:27 on the Pentateuch focuses on Abram/Abraham's descendants, the narrative begins with creation, Adam and Eve, and what happened to them and their descendants (Gen. 1:1–11:26). When the narrative shifts to Abram and identifies him as the son of Terah, who is the son of Shem, the son of Noah, the son of Seth, the son Adam, it not only links Abram with Adam, it also suggests that God's dealings with Abram continue the story of what happened after Adam and Eve were expelled from the garden for refusing divine instruction. With the Abram story the narrator continues to unfold the narrative problem of humanity's homelessness and its refusal of divine instruction by moving Abram toward God's presence as the result of divine instruction (Gen. 12:1–4a).

If this reading is correct, then Abram, too, like all of Adam's descendants, lived "east of Eden," exiled from the presence of God. When God instructs Abram to "leave your country, your people, and your father's household and go to the land I will show

2. On non-fulfillment as the theme of the Pentateuch, see David J. A. Clines, *The Theme of the Pentateuch*, 2nd ed., JSOTSup 10 (Sheffield: Sheffield Academic Press, 1997), and J. Severino Croatto, "Una promesa aun no cumplida. Algunos enfoques sobre la estructura del pentateuco," *Revista Bíblica* (Buenos Aires) 44 (1982): 193–206. Much of Croatto's article is summarized in his "The Function of the Non-fulfilled Promises: Reading the Pentateuch from the Perspective of the Latin-American Oppressed People," in Ingrid Rosa Kitzberger, ed., *The Personal Voice in Biblical Interpretation* (London: Routledge, 1999), 38–51.

you" (Gen. 12:1), the narrative begins to develop the solution to the problem it stated earlier, for from here on the narrative moves Abram and his descendants steadily toward that land where God would dwell in the midst of his people. Genesis 1:1–11:26, then, defines and develops the fundamental narrative problem: disobedient humanity's exile from the presence of God. Beginning with Genesis 11:27 the Pentateuch defines and develops a solution to humanity's problem, but now focused on a second human pair: Abram and Sarai. Like Adam and Eve, they too receive a fundamental instruction (Gen. 12:1–3).

### Adam-Eve and Abram-Sarai

The narrative's turn to Abram and Sarai highlights important similarities and differences between them and the first human pair, Adam and Eve.[3] Adam and Eve are parents of the entire human community, Abram and Sarai of a particular human community, one central to the narrator's interest; the community of which Adam and Eve are parents is characterized by its disobedient response to the word of the Lord in the garden; Abram and Sarai's descendants are shaped by Abram's obedient response to God's word in Genesis 12:1–3: "So Abram left" (Gen. 12:4a). There are also several differences. First, after God's speech Abram and Sarai no longer live "east of Eden"; they and their seed (Gen. 12:7) are on the way to the Promised Land. It is this "seed" that constitutes a second difference. Eve is the mother of all living (Gen. 3:20), and her progeny multiplies steadily generation after generation (Gen. 5:1–31; 11:10–26). This growth represents the effective blessing of Genesis 1:28 and 9:1, 7. Even in their flight from God's presence, the nations receive his blessings; but

---

3. Although the nations are rescued through Noah, God does not begin the redeemed community with him, nor does Noah's wife play a key role as do Eve and Sarai.

Israel's mother, Sarai, is barren (Gen. 11:30). Unlike the rest of humanity, she and Abram are incapable of generating a future. This points to the third difference: the community born of Abram and Sarai is not generated by the will of man but by the will of God (cf. John 1:13). In this particular community birth is not "natural"; it does not correspond merely to the creation order for humanity. Rather, among Abram's descendants birth is the counterpoint to barrenness. That is, the inability of that community to generate a future from its own "natural" biological resources, signaled by Sarai's barrenness (and other "mothers in Israel": Rebekah, Rachel, Samson's mother, Hannah), is overcome by divine intervention. Unlike the nations' growth, that of Abram's descendants corresponds uniquely to God's redemptive intervention, God's unique blessing upon his chosen people.[4] God's redemptive activity in and with Abram and his descendants points to a fourth difference: the Abram community, rooted in redemption, is instrumental for the redemptive blessing of the rest of the human community (Gen. 12:3b, 7; cf. Gal. 3:16).

Summarizing, by beginning with the garden of Eden and ending at the borders of the Promised Land the Pentateuch moves the reader from the expulsion from one place to the waiting for entry into another. And even though it is Israel that awaits entry into the land, and even though Israel is not a "natural" descendant of Adam, the links between Adam and Eve and Abram and Sarai and their descendants suggest that Israel rep-

---

4. The verb "to bless" occurs five times in Gen. 12:1–3. Through this blessing the Lord begins to undo the curses ('rr) declared in pre-Abram times (Gen. 3:14, 17; 4:11; 5:29; 9:25). On the blessing as a continuing reality in the creation and as shaped by salvation, see Claus Westermann, *Blessing in the Bible and the Life of the Church*, trans. Keith Crim, OBT (Philadelphia: Fortress, 1978), 1–14. Because of God's intervention in Sarai's barrenness, Nicodemus should have known (John 3:10) that birth among God's people is unique. Note also Ruth 4:13: "And she became his wife. And the LORD *enabled* her to conceive." Form-critical comparison with similar "conception" narratives discloses that "the LORD enabled" in Ruth 4:13 is unique.

resents the interests and needs of that community. "In Abram," then, "Adam" is awaiting entry to the land, and "in Abram" humanity's drift away from God has been turned around. But they are not yet in the land. The deficit of homelessness has not been completely canceled, for Adam's descendants "in Abram" continue in exile from the Promised Land as *the place* of God's presence. Nevertheless, by the end of the Pentateuch Israel is in a place that anticipates the land: the camp where she enjoys the *reality* of God's presence.

## Narrative Problem, Divine Instruction, and the Presence of God

The theme of God's presence receives its major exposition in Exodus with subsequent development in Leviticus and Numbers. In Exodus God brings Abraham's descendants to himself at Mt. Sinai (Ex. 19:4; cf. 3:12), makes a covenant with them, and instructs them in the design for his dwelling place (Ex. 25–31). After Israel constructs the various parts (Ex. 35–39) and Moses assembles and consecrates the tabernacle (Ex. 40:1–33), God dwells among his people (Ex. 40:34–35, cf. 25:8–9 and John 1:14). From the tabernacle God instructs Israel for clean and holy living in his presence (Lev. 1–27) and in how to organize the camp (Num. 1–10) so Israel will not defile the sanctuary (Lev. 20:3; cf. 15:31) or the camp "where I dwell among them" (Lev. 26:11; Num. 5:3; cf. 35:34; Deut. 23:14). Book by book the theme of God's presence is treated and developed. Genesis begins with a place consecrated by God's presence and shaped by his instructions, the garden of Eden; Exodus describes the design and construction of another place consecrated by God's presence; Leviticus and Numbers recall the instructions that shape life in God's presence on the way to the land; Deuteronomy repeats the basic instructions for sanctified living in God's presence in the land.

Looking at the theme of God's presence from the point of view of his instruction to Abraham to go to "the land I will show you," we note that from God's speech in Genesis 12:1–3 the narrative moves Abraham and his descendants—and the reader—toward the central place of God's presence in the Pentateuch, Sinai (Gen. 11:27–Ex. 18). There Israel receives instructions for building the sanctuary, for living holy lives in God's presence, and for organizing the camp with the sanctuary in the center (Ex. 19–40; Lev. 1–Num. 10). Being so instructed and in God's presence, Israel travels toward the land and arrives at the plains of Moab (Num. 11:1–22:1), where she remains for the rest of the narrative (Num. 22:2–36:13; Deut. 1:1–34:12). By the end of Deuteronomy the Pentateuch has resolved both aspects of its narrative problem: Adam's exiled descendants, by way of Abraham, dwell in a place shaped by the divine presence and instructions. Nevertheless, although the problem of exile from the presence of God has been solved, Israel has not yet received her promised rest in the land. The camp is not the land, but it anticipates and is a microcosm of the land.[5]

On the other side of the land experience, the exiles hear from Ezekiel that home is not tied to a specific earthly geography but to wherever God dwells: in the desert, the land, or even by the river Kebar. Similarly, the New Testament teaches that wherever the Holy Spirit indwells the two or three gathered in Christ's name (John 1:14), God is present. The Promised Land is not in itself the goal of God's redemption; the goal is to bring his chosen people into his presence. The following table illustrates the main elements of this movement in the biblical story line.

5. Compare "so they will not defile their *camp*, where I dwell among them" in Num. 5:3, with "Do not defile the *land* where you live and where I dwell" in Num. 35:34.

**Table 2.1 Development of the Pentateuch's storyline**

| Genesis | Exodus | Leviticus | Numbers | Deuter-onomy |
|---------|--------|-----------|---------|--------------|
| Exile from presence of God, the garden<br><br>Move toward Canaan | Move toward Sinai<br><br>Construction of tent at Sinai<br><br>Israel in presence of God | | Organization of the camp<br><br>Move from Sinai toward Canaan | |
| Failure to heed instruction (Adam and Eve)<br><br>Instruction to Abram and Sarai | | Instruction for living in God's holy presence, the tabernacle | | Repeated instructions for living in God's holy presence, the land |

The Pentateuch resolves the problem of humanity's defiant homelessness without recourse to the kind of place humanity would typically seek: soil sanctified by human presence, sweat, blood, and tears. Rather, the Pentateuch argues that the space God creates, indwells, and shapes by his instructions is humanity's true home. And, although the Promised Land will be such a place, it is not a permanent resting place, so Israel must be careful to live in it by the Lord's instructions (Lev. 18:1–5) and not transform the land itself into the primary goal. Abraham's descendants receive Canaan as their inheritance, but only for a time. This comports with her origins: Israel was born of barren Sarai. From the beginning God created her; she is not the product solely of human biology. Thus Israel must not make her own physical descent the prime criterion of her identity. Similarly with the physical place of her temporary dwelling. Adam's other grandchildren will join Israel, as did Rahab, Ruth, and Naaman; but the place of God's dwelling will be rebuilt (John 2:19–20) and established far beyond the Promised Land, for Abraham's offspring will inherit the earth.[6]

### The Scope of the Pentateuch: Torah, Divine Instruction in the Presence of God

Approximately one-third of the Pentateuch's narrative time is dedicated to Israel's stay at Sinai. Throughout this time Moses instructs Israel: for construction of the Lord's dwelling place; for sacrifices, cleanliness, and holiness; in the arrangement of the camp for its journey toward the land. Abraham's descendants arrive at Sinai untutored in the ways of God; they leave it fully instructed in cleanliness and experienced in God's holiness. Moses' instructions at Sinai form the scope of the Pentateuch for through them Moses addresses the fundamental problem defined in the beginning: refusal of divine instruction and exile from the presence of God.

Israel's stay at Sinai is the time of her instruction in the holiness and cleanliness that permits her to live in God's presence. Sinai's narrative antecedents instruct Israel in the separation from the rebellious nations (Babel and Egypt) that identifies Abram and his descendants. The post-Sinai narrative instructs Israel in the first generation's response to and consequences of disregarding divine instruction and the Lord's challenge of loyalty to the second generation (Numbers). She must remember divine

6. Paul's use of the Greek *kosmos* in Rom. 4:13 plays on the Hebrew *'erets*, which means both land and earth.

instruction when she enters the land—the place of God's presence—and not forget it (Deut. 8). Deuteronomy places all this under the rubric of "this law" (*htwrh hz't*: Deut. 1:5; 4:44; 17:18, 19, etc.). The Pentateuch combines narrative and instruction such that when the reading community finishes Deuteronomy it has been reminded of its fundamental identity: a people fully instructed to live in God's presence, awaiting entry into the fullness of the Promised Land (cf. Heb. 4:1–13).

Textually embodied and fixed in the received narrative, the divine voice from Sinai continues to define God's people and the place she lives, wherever that may be: the Promised Land, exile (Josh. 1:6–9; 23:6–7; Ezek. 18), or the dispersion (1 Peter 1:1; James 1:1). That voice also prohibits them from living by instruction from Egypt or Canaan (Lev. 18:1–5), and forbids the development of an autochthonous theology in Canaan (Ex. 23:23–26). The voice is God's, the messenger is Moses. In Deuteronomy, to hear Moses is to hear God. Moses is the scope of the Pentateuch. The same divine voice speaks authoritatively through Jesus Christ, the Son of God, whose ministry embodied a life of holiness by submitting to his Father's instruction (John 17). To hear Christ is to hear the Father; to hear the voice at Sinai as embedded in the Pentateuch is to hear the voice of the Father of Jesus Christ; and the Father, according to Matthew, tells us: "Listen to him [Jesus]" (Matt. 17:5).

## The Structure of the Pentateuch

The structure of the Pentateuch did not become a debated issue until scholarship reconstructed it along source-, form-, and tradition-critical lines, thereby rejecting the traditional five-fold division. As a result, it became common to speak of the Sinai pericope (Ex. 19–Num. 10) even without reference to its source-critical

33

origins or consequences. Nevertheless, the observation is useful: Israel's long stay at Sinai emphasizes the central role of divine instruction in God's presence, a centrality supported by the frame of two desert journeys, one to Sinai (Ex. 15:21–18:27) and the other away from it (Num. 10:11–22:1). This segmentation of the Pentateuch fails, however, to respect the received division of the Pentateuch into five sub-units, with the consequence that Leviticus' unique form of holiness instruction is easily over-looked. When we do follow the traditional division in linear sequence, allowing each of the major narrative units its unique contribution to the presentation and resolution of the funda-mental narrative problem, we find that holiness instruction is still the central concern of the Pentateuch, but now in the form of a received book: Leviticus.

In the concentric[7] organization of the Pentateuch parallels between Exodus and Numbers suggest that they constitute a frame for Leviticus. Parallels between Genesis and Deuteronomy not only frame Exodus–Leviticus–Numbers thematically, they also provide the beginning and conclusion to the linear sequence of the entire pentateuchal narrative. Thus, Genesis through Deu-teronomy exhibits an $ABCB^1A^1$ organizational format in which Deuteronomy returns to and complements the themes of Gen-esis, and Numbers returns to and complements the themes of Exodus. This leaves Leviticus occupying the narrative center of the Pentateuch, as illustrated in the chart below.

7. See Mark S. Smith, "Matters of Space and Time in Exodus and Numbers," in *Theological Exegesis: Essays in Honor of Brevard S. Childs*, ed. Christopher Seitz and Kathryn Green-McGreight (Grand Rapids: Eerdmans: 1999), 201–7; Erich Zenger, et. al., *Einleitung in das Alte Testament* (Stuttgart: Kohlhammer, 1995), 36–39; and my "An Iconography of Order: Kingship in Exodus" (ThD dissertation, University of Toronto, 1992), 350–70. Yehuda T. Radday ("Chiasm in Tora," *Linguistica Biblica* 19 [1972]: 21–22) argues that biblical authors placed the central thought of a text in the middle.

**Table 2.2 Leviticus as the center of the Pentateuch**

| | | | |
|---|---|---|---|
| **A—Genesis** | Separation from the nations<br><br>Blessing<br><br>Seeing the land<br><br>Descendants and the land | | |
| **B—Exodus** | | Israel's desert journeys<br><br>Apostasy and plagues<br><br>Pharaoh and magicians<br><br>First-born/ Levites | |
| **C—Leviticus** | | | Sacrifices<br><br>Cleanliness<br><br>Holiness |
| **B¹—Numbers** | | Israel's desert journeys<br><br>Apostasy and plagues<br><br>Balak and Balaam<br><br>First-born/ Levites | |
| **A¹— Deuteronomy** | Separation from the nations<br><br>Blessing<br><br>Seeing the land<br><br>Descendants and the land | | |

# Leviticus as the Narrative *axis mundi* of the Pentateuch

Leviticus' central narrative role has been obscured for a variety of reasons: interest in the mighty acts of God in history (Leviticus has none), dislike of things ritual (Leviticus has it all), its submersion into the Sinai pericope. As a collection of sacrificial, cleanliness, and holiness instructions with narrative scattered throughout in introductions to speeches (Lev. 8–10 and 24:1–23), Leviticus easily distinguishes itself from Exodus and Numbers. Leviticus' opening narrative line, nevertheless, links it to the antecedent narrative (Ex. 40:34–38, esp. vv. 34–35) and thus to the building and covenant narrative with instructions from Sinai. In addition, the opening narrative line introduces divine speech from the Tent of Meeting, the meeting place that has replaced Sinai as the locus of divine self-disclosure. Given this narrative link, what is the relationship between the instructions of Leviticus and the building and covenant instructions with narrative in Exodus?

Covenant instruction in Exodus 19–24 and 34 expresses the nature and extent of the suzerain-vassal relationship to which Israel has bound herself by self-maledictory oath. Levitical instruction, and the tabernacle instruction so closely linked to it, although embedded within the previously established covenant relationship, is nonetheless of a fundamentally different character. Building and priestly instruction do not primarily seek to bind a community in loyalty but to organize the vassal community already bound by oath to the speaker, by means of a ritual center, ritual instructions, and rituals themselves. Refusal to submit to such instruction and ritual, intentional or not, occasions uncleanness, expulsion from the presence of God, or death (Ex. 32:10, 35; Lev. 10:1–3; 12; 13:46; 24:10–23). In the terms of the Pentateuch's fundamental narrative problem, obedience to Levitical instruction and maintenance of the ritual at the ritual center keeps Israel safe in God's presence; it prevents the exile, uncleanness, and death that are the natural inheritance of Adam's descendants. The instructions of Leviticus "fill out" the space where Israel lives in God's presence. Even as God designed the creation and organized it for blessed and holy habitation in his presence, and as he designed his own dwelling place, so the Lord shapes the space occupied by his people in his presence. All this he does for his people's benefit. Frank H. Gorman writes:

> Sacred space has been constructed according to the pattern given by Yahweh; it is now necessary to detail the form of activity that is to take place in the sacred space. Just as Yahweh gave instructions for the construction of sacred space, Yahweh now gives instruction for the ritual that is to take place in that sacred structure.

He continues:

> Defilement of the sanctuary is of such concern to the Priestly writers because it threatens the integrity of sacred space, the dwelling place of Yahweh. Thus defilement of the tabernacle threatens to drive Yahweh from the midst of Israel. It is Yahweh's dwelling in the tabernacle that is of crucial theological importance for the Priestly writers. It is one constitutive element of their notion of order. Thus, sacred space must be protected and cleansed when necessary in order to maintain Yahweh's presence in the holy of holies.[8]

8. Frank H. Gorman Jr., *The Ideology of Ritual: Space, Time and Status in the Priestly Theology* (Sheffield: JSOT, 1990), 48, 51. While it is ultimately true to say that defilement of the tabernacle drives the Lord from Israel's midst, as we see in Ezek. 8–10, in Leviticus defilement drives Israel from the Lord's presence, outside the camp.

37

Located after the successful assembly and indwelling of the tabernacle—the monument to the Lord's cosmic rule—the divine instruction of Leviticus describes the manner in which Israel's cult and conduct will manifest that rule on the way to the land, and subsequently in the land itself. That is, even though the sanctuary itself is crucial as the Lord's dwelling place, the instructional and ritual order of Leviticus focuses on the cleanness and holiness of Israel as a people in whose midst the Lord dwells, thereby anticipating Paul's discussion of the body of Christ as the temple of the Holy Spirit.

It is the people, then, gathered in the presence of God[9] who by their loyal submission to the Levitical instruction embody the Lord's victory over the disorder of the nations and so proclaim his cosmic rule; they are the ongoing memorial. This accords with the purpose of the sanctuary as enunciated in Exodus 25:8 and 29:45, 46: The Lord will dwell among *them* (*btwkm*), and in Leviticus: "You must keep the Israelites separate from things that make them unclean, so they will not die in their uncleanness for defiling my dwelling place, which is among *them*" (Lev. 15:31; cf. 26:11 and Num. 5:3; 35:34). The sanctuary is the means by which God becomes "incarnate" in Israel's midst, but it is Israel herself who is the goal of this incarnation, not only because God wants to dwell *among them*, but because by means of submission to the instructional and ritual order she will embody the cleanliness and holiness required for God to dwell in her midst, ultimately without the aid of a building (John 2:21; 1 Cor. 3:16; 6:19; 2 Cor. 7:1).

9. "It is this presence which imposes upon man a quite definite behaviour." Gerhard von Rad, *Old Testament Theology: The Theology of the Historical Traditions*, trans. D. M. G. Stalker (New York: Harper & Row, 1962), 242. Although he is commenting on Exodus 19:5, 6, Dale Patrick writes that "Israel is like a sanctuary in the midst of a profane world," in his *Old Testament Law* (Atlanta: John Knox, 1985), 231.

In its central location Leviticus forms the climax of the instructions at Sinai; through its detailed instructions it opens up the meaning of Exodus 19:5–6: Israel is fundamentally a priestly people. It also reflects a resolution to the fundamental problem defined at the beginning of the Pentateuch: by submitting to the instructions of Leviticus in the Lord's presence Israel will do what Adam and Eve refused to do in the garden. Obedience to this instruction will bring about a moral order different from that of the nations (Egypt and Canaan, Lev. 18:1–5); refusal of this instruction, whether for its chosen priests (Lev. 10:1–3) or the priestly people (Lev. 24:10–23; 26:14–39), will occasion death, uncleanness, and exile, from the camp or the land.

Like the tabernacle and later the temple (cf. Isa. 2:2–3), Leviticus forms a narrative center for the textual community, the people of God. After the Pentateuch depicts the defiled nations' unyielding moving away from the Lord's presence, it takes Abram and his descendants steadfastly toward the Lord's presence at Sinai where, especially in the speeches of Leviticus, they receive life-giving instruction in cleanliness and holiness. In Leviticus the textual community, God's people of all ages, hears about and identifies itself with the people rescued from the chaos and uncleanness of the nations to accompany the Lord on his royal military campaign as he moves toward Canaan.[10] At this place, Sinai, Israel is at home, for she is in

---

10. "From ancient time almost to the present day it has been customary to begin teaching children not from *Genesis* but from *Vayikra*—the laws of the sacrifices." N. Leibowitz, *Studies in Vayikra* (Jerusalem: The World Zionist Organization, 1983), 3. This choice reflects the concern for order typical of the ancient Near East; see Othmar Keel, *The Symbolism of the Biblical World: Ancient Near Eastern Iconography and the Book of Psalms*, trans. Timothy J. Hallett (New York: Seabury, 1978), 16–60. Compare this to the tendency to begin reading the Pentateuch with Exodus, which reflects the concern for history as the primary category.

God's presence. At this textual center, Leviticus, Israel receives instructions for organizing her life in the presence of God. Being safely in God's presence, Israel now awaits entry into the Promised Land.

## Summary and Conclusions

The ultimate goal of the Lord's redemptive intervention in human affairs, beginning with his instructions to Abram in Genesis 12, is the reestablishment of the moral order—in place since creation but rejected by Adam's descendants—in the land of Canaan (Gen. 12:1; Ex. 3:8, 17; Deut. 34:4). Exodus describes a divine military campaign against a particular instance of rebellious human response to the cosmic order, the covenant with Abraham's rescued descendants at Sinai, and the establishment of a separate sacred space to memorialize the Lord's victory (Ex. 29:43–46). Leviticus fills that separated space with the appropriate ritual and moral order. Numbers takes the Lord's divisions to the borders of Canaan, but not without first instructing the second generation in the importance of maintaining the camp's purity and the consequences of its defilement. Deuteronomy, addressed to Israel on the plains of Moab, reminds the second generation to execute the military campaign begun in Exodus in submission to divine instruction. Proper execution of these instructions in Canaan will prompt the blessing the Lord originally intended for the entire human community (Gen. 1:28; cf. 12:3).

In the Pentateuch Israel never enters into the land; this remains a future reality that shapes Abraham's and Israel's journey with God from Ur to the plains of Moab. Each of the pentateuchal books, however, provides a unique perspective on Israel's waiting for the land. This juxtaposition of the present condition and a future reality is crucial for a people languishing in exile and for those waiting in the post-resurrection dispersion. It reinforces the truth that home is not defined by a particular physical geography, but a spiritual presence and a teaching voice. That is the message of the Pentateuch for God's people of all ages who are waiting for the land.

# 3

## Narrative Coherence
## and Conceptual Pattern
## of the Pentateuch

The concentric shape of the Pentateuch lends it a formal coherence that allows the reader to appreciate it as a literary unit with unified interests; the linear sequence provides coherence by bringing the fundamental problem to a resolution, albeit incomplete. In this chapter we will consider the narrative coherence of the Pentateuch from the point of view of its conceptual pattern.

### Narrative Coherence and
### the Kingship Pattern

Royal language is a pervasive metaphor in the Pentateuch. Expressed in a well-known pattern—a king who, when confronted with disorder in his kingdom, seeks out the enemy, defeats him, and upon returning to his capital builds a structure in celebration of his victory—this metaphor illuminates the conceptual coherence of the Pentateuch. The pattern is most clearly demonstrated in the extra-biblical Enuma Elish and Baal epics.[1] These epics and other accounts of royal victory and temple building[2] suggest that this pattern is a well-known literary configuration with cosmological significance. The importance of this conceptual pattern has been recognized and applied to the Genesis account of creation, Exodus 15, Psalms 74 and 89, and Isaiah 40–55,[3] but its relevance for the Pentateuch has not yet been explored. The epics illustrate the pattern as follows.

1. I am not arguing for material literary dependence, but for similarity of sequence. Isaac M. Kikawada suggests something similar. There are, he writes, "more than a thousand years of literary tradition preceding the compilation of the biblical narrative during which the double creation story is used to preface the early history of mankind that climaxed in the great flood," in his "The Double Creation of Mankind in *Enki and Nimhah, Atrahasis I 1–351* and *Genesis 1–2*," *Iraq* 45 (1983): 45. Alexander Heidel argues that the sequence of events in Enuma Elish and Gen. 1:1–2:3 were similar, in his *The Babylonian Genesis: The Story of Creation*, 2nd ed. (Chicago: University of Chicago Press, 1969).

2. For example, the temple for Shamash built by Yahdun-Lin after defeating rebel vassals, *ANETSup*, 120–21; the temple built by Innana, at Agade, after Enlil had defeated Uruk, in Jerrold S. Cooper, *The Curse of Agade* (Baltimore: The John Hopkins University Press, 1983), 51, 11.1–9; and the temple of Gatumdug after the defeat of Ur, in Jerrold S. Cooper, *Sumerian and Akkadian Royal Inscriptions*, PreSargonic Inscriptions 1 (New Haven: The American Oriental Society, 1986), 43, 45. For a study on the relationship between ancient Near Eastern temples and the biblical temple see V. Hurowitz, *I Have Built You an Exalted House*, JSOTSup 115 (Sheffield: Sheffield Academic Press, 1992).

3. "The cosmogonic myths of kingship and salvation through the work of the divine warrior have . . . profoundly molded the *conceptual pattern* of early Israel as reflected in her poetry." Patrick D. Miller, *The Divine Warrior in Early Israel* (Cambridge: Harvard Press, 1973), 117 (emphasis added). See also Bernhard W. Anderson, *Creation versus Conflict: The Reinterpretation of Mythical Symbolism in the Bible* (Philadelphia: Fortress, 1987), 11–42; Peter C. Craigie, "The Poetry of Ugarit and Israel," *TynBul* 22 (1971): 3–31, esp. 19–24; Paul D. Hanson, *The Dawn of Apocalyptic: The Historical and Sociological Roots of Jewish Apocalyptic Eschatology* (Philadelphia: Fortress, 1979), 292–334; William R. Millar, *Isaiah 24–27 and the Origin of the Apocalyptic* (Missoula: Scholars Press, 1976), 71–81; Tryggve N. D. Mettinger, "In Search of the Hidden Structure: YHWH as King in Isaiah 40–55," *SEÅ* 51–52 (1986–1987): 153.

**Enuma Elish**

1. *The occasion for the conflict*: Tiamat's revenge for Apsu's death; Marduk will fight for supreme authority.
2. *The kingship*: Kingship is bestowed.
3. *The battle*: Marduk defeats Tiamat with a war-bow; salvation of the gods.
4. *The palace*: Building of the temple Esharra; bricks made for one year; erected at beginning of second year; Marduk sits down in majesty; a victory banquet. Marduk's rule; praise of kingship and proclamation of the fifty names.

**Baal and Yamm**

1. *The occasion for the conflict*: Yam's messengers demand Baal's tribute; Ashtarte urges Baal to seize the eternal kingship.
2. *The battle*: Baal battles Yamm; Baal defeats Yamm with a club.
3. *The kingship*: Baal's kingship is proclaimed; the victory banquet. Complaints: no house for Baal; Baal travels to Mt. Zaphon.
4. *The palace*: A dwelling for Baal requested; Anat brings news of permission; House of Baal will be the size of Mt. Zaphon and will be built by Kothar and Hasis. A victory banquet and Baal's rule. The palace is the place from which Baal speaks.

Although both epics contain the same major elements in similar patterns there are some differences: Marduk's kingship is proclaimed before the battle and the description of Baal's palace construction is more extensive. Extant royal inscriptions recall the king's heroic deeds, but do not regularly mention conflict as a precedent for the building of a temple. Nevertheless, Tadmor has shown that even when such inscriptions change their format they continue to function as ideological expressions of royal rule.[4] Later inscriptions extol the king's might through his building accomplishments alone; his heroic deeds are not mentioned.[5] Thus, although these literary and historiographical conventions were not strictly limited to a particular sequence they were regularly used to communicate the image the king wanted to project.[6] The pattern's movement from the place of conflict back to the center of the empire where the victor would build a temple, palace, or other monument in public recognition of the god's blessing on the successful venture, reinforces its cosmological significance.

Comparison between Exodus and the ancient epics discloses several differences. Thus, the Lord builds his own palace, but Baal needs El's consent. The Lord's people craft the tabernacle and voluntarily contribute the gold and silver (Ex. 35:5, 22; 36:2); in the Baal epic the gods' craftsman, *Kothar wa Hassis*, does all the work and the materials were generally brought in from distant mountains.[7] Finally, where in the ancient Near East temples were considered a resting place for the gods,[8] in Exodus

4. Hayim Tadmor, "History and Ideology in the Assyrian Royal Inscriptions," in *Assyrian Royal Inscriptions: New Horizons in Literary, Ideological, and Historical Analysis*, OAC 17 (Rome: Istituto Per L'Oriente, 1981), 14, 29.

5. Ibid., 24.

6. Ibid., 14.

7. Gudea brought the materials from the Cedar mountain, having made paths and quarries where no one had gone before. "Gudea cylinders a and b," *ANET*, 268–69. Eanatum brought white cedar from the mountains, Cooper, *Sumerian and Akkadian Royal Inscriptions*, 49. Bringing in such materials and the finest crafts from the periphery to the cosmic center represents the completeness of creation at its center: "at the center of the world there is everything, all is known, all is possessed—creation is complete." Mario Liverani, "The Ideology of the Assyrian Empire," in *Power and Propaganda*, Copenhagen Studies in Assyriology 7 (Copenhagen: Akademisk Forlag, 1979), 314. See also *ANET*, 275–76.

8. M. Weinfeld, "Sabbath, Temple and the Enthronement of the Lord—the Problem of the Sitz im Leben of Genesis 1:1–2:3," 502n2, in A. Caquot and

the *mškn* is only the means for the Lord's dwelling in the midst of his people (Ex. 25:8: "in *their* midst" ESV) and later leading his people. In spite of these differences the elements of this pattern are recognizable in Exodus.[9]

1. *The occasion for conflict*: Pharaoh's oppression (Ex. 1–2:25); the Lord's messengers demand Pharaoh's submission (Ex. 3:1–7:7).
2. *The battle*: The conflict (Ex. 7:8–11:10): the exodus (Ex. 12:1–13:16); Pharaoh's defeat (Ex. 13:17–14:31).
3. *The kingship*: The Lord's victory and proclamation of kingship (Ex. 15:1–21); the Lord takes Israel to Mt. Sinai (Ex. 15:22–19:2); the Lord makes Israel his people (Ex. 19:3–24:11).
4. *The palace*: the Lord will dwell among Israel (Ex. 24:12–25:9); building instructions (Ex. 25:10–31:18); Israel's rebellion (Ex. 32:1–34:35); tabernacle and furniture crafted (Ex. 35–39:31); Moses inspects the work and blesses the people (Ex. 39:42–43); Moses instructed to set up *mškn* on first day of second year (Ex. 40:1–2); Moses sets up the tabernacle in seven acts (Ex. 40:17–33); the Lord dwells in the *mškn* (Ex. 40:34–38).

These elements do not so much structure as illuminate the coherence of the narrative in terms of a well-known cultural pattern. Thus, the conflict between God and Pharaoh is resolved and the reality of God's rule and his victory is sung in Exodus 15:1–21. Thereafter Israel, as God's military divisions, travels through the

M. Delcor, eds., *Melange bibliques et orientaux en l'honneur de Henri Cazalles*, AOAT 212 (Neukirchen-Vluyn: Neukirchener Verlag, 1981), 501–12.

9. Arie C. Leder, "The Coherence of Exodus: Narrative Unity and Meaning," *CTJ* 36 (2001): 251–69.

desert to Sinai, a journey not unlike the return to the empire's ideological center of the great armies of an ancient overlord such as Shalmaneser III or Assurnasirpal.[10] At Sinai the Lord's victory over Egypt is formalized with a suzerain-vassal treaty. There a new theme begins with the Lord's instructions for the tabernacle, the royal throne room, which embodies the Lord's victory and rule in Israel's midst. This structure replaces the mountain as cultic and symbolic center after the glory-cloud fills the tabernacle.[11]

Elements of the kingship pattern also illuminate the other books of the Pentateuch: Genesis anticipates and prepares for the complete pattern in Exodus, after which Leviticus, Numbers, and Deuteronomy may be read as varying expositions of the building element of the pattern.

## The Kingship Pattern and the Pentateuch

Genesis 1:1–2:3 depicts the Creator and his creation in royal and priestly terms.[12] Because all of creation is the Lord's kingdom

10. Israel's depicted military journey through the desert has analogues in the royal annals of Shalmaneser III and Assurnasirpal where itineraries depict royal military marches with river crossings, problems of finding water, military exploits, hunting, and the receiving of tribute. See Graham I. Davies, "The Wilderness Itineraries: A Comparative Study," *TynBul* 25 (1974): 58. In the same article Davis argues that "the itineraries comparable to Numbers 33:1–49 from the Ancient Near East relate exclusively, so far as our evidence goes, to royal military campaigns. It may therefore be due to the conception of the wilderness period as a military expedition that an account of it in the form of an itinerary was composed," 80. For further studies on these itineraries as royal military marches see George W. Coats, "The Wilderness Itinerary," *CBQ* 34 (1972): 147–48; Graham I. Davies, "The Wilderness Itineraries and the Composition of the Pentateuch," *VT* 33 (1983): 1–13.

11. On temples and mountains as cosmic centers, see Othmar Keel, *The Symbolism of the Biblical World: Ancient Near Eastern Iconography and the Book of Psalms*, trans. Timothy J. Hallett (New York: Seabury, 1978), 113–20.

12. See John H. Stek, "What Says the Scripture?" in *Portraits of Creation: Biblical and Scientific Perspective on the World's Formation*, ed. Howard J. Van Till et al. (Grand

and all creatures his subjects, they enjoy life and good order in his presence. Disorder intrudes with Adam and Eve's refusal of the divine instructions, for which they are expelled from the presence of the King. From now on this ancestral pair and their descendants cannot escape the chaos they have brought upon themselves. Covetousness (3:6), fratricide (4:8), vengeance (4:23– 24), and wickedness (6:5) characterize the post-fall world such that the Creator determines to cleanse it. Destructive waters swallow the earth and its inhabitants, except for righteous Noah, his family, and selected animals. After the waters return to their assigned places, Noah receives instructions for righteous living (9:1–7). All seems to be in order.

But post-flood peoples breed chaos again and build a city with a tower to reach the heavens (11:1–9), a place denied to mere humanity. Babel's arrogance is followed by the Lord's selection of Abram, with whom he begins to address the roots of this disorder and its consequences. By choosing Abram, the King for a time abandons the nations—although they are in constant contact (Abraham and Pharaoh, the kings of the plains, Sodom and Gomorrah, Abimelech; Isaac and Abimelech; Jacob and Shechem; Joseph, and later the entire patriarchal family, in Egypt). The Lord swears treaties with Abram; through them he promises to cancel the deficit of the refusal of divine instruction, undo the expulsion from his presence, and overcome the disorder. The element of the kingship pattern which shapes Genesis is the

---

Rapids: Eerdmans, 1990), 232–35. Gordon J. Wenham ("Sanctuary Symbolism in the Garden of Eden Story," *Proceedings of the World Congress of Jewish Studies* 9 [1986]: 1925) argues that the opening chapters of Genesis depict the creation as a sanctuary and humanity as a priestly pair. This comports with the ANE view of sacral kingship. See E. O. James, "The Sacred Kingship and the Priesthood," *The Sacral Kingship: Studies in the History of Religions* 4 (Leiden: Brill, 1959), 63–70; Sigmund Mowinckel, "General Oriental and Specific Elements in the Israelite Conception of the Sacral Kingdom," in *The Sacral Kingship: Studies in the History of Religions* 4 (Leiden: Brill, 1959), 283–94.

intrusion of chaos among the nations (2:4–11:26), occasioned by the conflict between the ancestral human pair and God (2:15–17; 3:1–8). The great flood is nothing less than the Great King's royal military response. After the flood waters return to their assigned places, the Lord begins a military march with Abram, one that will, in the fullness of the time, defeat the great proponent of disorder (Col. 2:15).

Exodus continues the theme of the nations' rebellion in the person of Pharaoh. Pharaoh forces Abram's descendants, covenant servants of the Lord (Gen. 17), to build his store cities in a foolish attempt to prevent Israel from serving God. He succeeds only in getting into trouble with Israel's God. Although he makes life miserable for God's people, Pharaoh's attempt to "swallow" Israel ultimately fails; chaos itself is swallowed up in victory (7:8–13; 15:17; cf. Isa. 25:8; 1 Cor. 15:54).[13] Israel leaves Egypt and swears a suzerain-vassal covenant with the Great King at Mt. Sinai, where he instructs his servants in the design and construction of a mobile palace, which will be the earthly center of the Lord's rule. The King then indwells the tabernacle, a building Israel constructed for him, not for Pharaoh. At this point in the narrative, Adam's descendants by way of Abraham find themselves in God's presence.

All the elements of the kingship pattern are present in Exodus: the occasion for conflict, response to the conflict and subsequent victory, and the building of a memorial: the Great King's palace. After the glory of the Lord indwells the tabernacle it, as the building element of the kingship pattern, lends coherence to Leviticus and Numbers.

Leviticus explains the building element further, especially Exodus 25:8: "have them make a sanctuary for me, and I will

---

13. See my "Hearing Exodus 7:8–13 to Preach the Gospel: The Ancient Adversary in Today's World," *CTJ* 43 (2008): 93–110.

dwell among *them*." The tabernacle is the means for God to dwell among his people; that is the goal of the Sinai construction project. But the tabernacle is a only a temporary instrument for the Lord's dwelling among his people (John 2:20). For that reason the Lord speaks from the Tent of Meeting to instruct his *people* to live sacrificial, clean, and holy lives. Israel itself will be the "building" from which God rules the nations. As an exposition of Israel's priestly character (Ex. 19:6), Leviticus anticipates Christ's dwelling among his people, the church, his body, "living stones . . . being built into a spiritual house to be a holy priesthood" (1 Peter 2:5; and John 1:14; 2:12–22). In their holiness and cleanliness, God's own people are a living memorial to the Lord's victory over Egypt and are emblematic of his, not Pharaoh's, universal rule.

Where Leviticus treats Israel herself as a living memorial to God's victory and rule, Numbers focuses on the physical camp, more specifically, an armed military camp with the Great King's throne room at its center (Num. 2:17). The army of the Lord escorts the enthroned Great King on his victory march from Sinai to the Promised Land; they will leave Sinai at his command through Moses (10:13, 35). As in Leviticus, so in Numbers, cleanliness is crucial for life in the camp (5:3) as it will be in the land (35:34). But, Israel, understood to be the Lord's army since Exodus (12:41, 51; 13:18), and successfully so against Amalek (Ex. 17:8–16), refuses to engage the Canaanites and suffers the fate of a rebellious army: execution. Ironically, it is what they fearfully wished for (14:2). The generation that saw God's mighty acts in Egypt will not enter the Promised Land (14:22); their children will (14:31). Forty long years they will wander the desert wastes until death overcomes all the rebels (14:34).

The Lord's armies have success against Sihon and Og, and the Lord ensures a blessing to counter Balak's attempts at cursing, but

Israel brings upon herself a deadly plague consequent upon its apostasy with the Baal of Peor (Num. 25). By the end of Numbers, God's army, now composed of second-generation Israelites, awaits entry on the plains of Moab. There Moses challenges them not to repeat the unfaithfulness of the first generation nor "to defile the land where you [will] live and where I dwell, for I, the LORD, dwell among the Israelites" (35:34; cf. 5:3). Thus the royal escort of the memorial of the Lord's victory awaits its promised future.[14]

Deuteronomy addresses the second generation in the light of the Numbers' mutiny and enlarges upon their task when it enters into contact with the nations in the Promised Land. Two aspects of Moses' speeches contribute to the pattern: Israel's military task of destroying all the Canaanites who, as Adam and Eve's descendants, are disloyal to the Great King's rule; and the speeches as "this law" (*htwrh hz't*: Deut. 1:5; etc.): royal instruction which the second generation is to embody in its ridding the land of the nations, and in its cult and conduct. Thus they will memorialize the Lord's victory and rule. The challenge before Israel is to remain loyal to the Lord, to remember God's leading in the desert once they have entered the land, not to engage in cultic acts which honor "other gods," only to worship at the place which the Lord chooses, and not to intermarry, lest the spouse's other gods subvert Israel's loyalty.

Recognition of these elements of the kingship pattern integrates Deuteronomy into the Pentateuch by a sustained emphasis on submission to "this law" and the temple as the

---

14. The kingship pattern also lends conceptual coherence to the desert journey in Numbers. Positively, it depicts Israel on a royal military expedition that began on Passover night (Ex. 12:51), one that has some success. Negatively, however, the first generation army commits mutiny by refusing to enter the Promised Land, thereby endangering the journey to the promised future.

place of the Lord's instruction. By submission to "this law," especially with respect to the centrality of the temple, Israel will embody the Lord's victory over the disorder that threatens, and his rule over the nations. Deuteronomy also addresses the future potential of Israel's rebellion against God in the land, the consequent eruption of disorder in a land shaped by "this law," her joining in the generation of the chaos of the nations, and the consequences: an infertile land and expulsion from the presence of God. Deuteronomy then, focuses on two elements of the pattern: disorder and building.

## The Coherence and Meaning of the Pattern

The kingship pattern does not structure but underscores the coherence of the Pentateuch and provides a key to its meaning. This meaning can best be understood from the perspective of the manner in which the pattern illuminates the meaning and coherence of Exodus.

### Exodus

The pattern lends Exodus coherence for four reasons. First, Exodus employs all the elements of the pattern in telling its story and in so doing accounts for the entire narrative, unlike the lamentation liturgy, suggested by Plastaras and Westermann, which accounts only for Exodus 1:1–15:21.[15] The conflict between God and Pharaoh and Egypt's ultimate demise, the Sinai legislation, the building instructions, the rebellion, and ultimately the compliance with the instructions all fit within the development of the kingship pattern. Second, because the pattern reaches its

15. See below chap 5, fn. 14.

climax in a building project, it reinforces the contrastive literary frame of Exodus: the building of Pharaoh's store cities in Exodus 1 and the construction of the Great King's earthly dwelling place in Exodus 35:4–40:33. In this connection it is important to note that the Hebrew *'bdh* is used to describe two projects: Israel's work on the tabernacle (39:32, 42) and her work on the store cities (1:14 ["slavery," 2:23; 6:9]). The difference between the two narrative situations is that Pharaoh forced Israel to build his cities, whereas the Lord's forgiveness led Israel voluntarily (Ex. 35:21; 36:6b) to participate in the construction of the tabernacle. In addition, and related to the former, the fourth element of the pattern, the building project, coincides with the narrative's cancellation of the deficit. Third, the elements of the pattern naturally link the tabernacle section to the preceding events that took place in Egypt, the desert, and at Mt. Sinai, as well as both covenant and tabernacle instructions. This produces a coherent narrative. In a cultural context where the kingship pattern was prevalent, it would only be natural to read, after consolidating the victory at Sinai, that the victorious king engaged in a construction project to memorialize the event in some way.

Finally, the kingship pattern also lends conceptual coherence to Exodus by rendering explicit the meaning implicit in the royal metaphor that shapes Exodus throughout. This is especially clear in the use of the noun "king," applied to Pharaoh but never to the Lord; his royal status is indicated only in the clause "The Lord will reign" (Ex. 15:18). The Lord's kingship does not, of course, depend on the title; his actions disclose who he is. Only a Great King could have done to Pharaoh and Egypt what he did. The kingship pattern supports his status not only in the conflict with Egypt, but also in the rest of the narrative, including Israel's survival in the desert where God's divisions travel to Mt. Sinai, the center of God's earthly kingdom in the Pentateuch.

## The Pentateuch as a Whole

The completion of the kingship pattern in Exodus 40 evokes the deficit with which the biblical narrative begins in Genesis: Adam and Eve expelled from God's presence in the garden of Eden. When the glory cloud fills the newly constructed tabernacle God dwells in the midst of the descendants of Adam and Eve, those born, miraculously, of Abram and barren Sarai. Adam's descendants are in God's presence not because they found their own way back, but because God has brought them to himself (Ex. 19:4). Moreover, they are not in his immediate presence; Israel's sinfulness requires a distance (Ex. 19:13; cf. Num. 1:53) which can only be overcome by a specially appointed priesthood (Ex. 29:1; Num. 18:1–7; cf. Heb. 9:19–25). The elements of the text that point us in this direction are the phrases in Exodus 39 and 40 that recall the creation narrative.[16]

**Table 3.1 Comparison of creation and tabernacle narratives**

| | |
|---|---|
| Thus the heavens and the earth were *completed* . . . By the seventh day God had *finished* the *work* he had been doing (Gen. 2:1-2). | So all the work on the tabernacle was *completed*. (Ex. 39:32); And so Moses *finished* the *work*. (Ex. 40:33) |
| God *saw* all that he had made, and (behold, [*hnh*]) it was very good. (Gen. 1:31). | Moses inspected the work and *saw* (behold, [*hnh*]) they had done it just as the LORD had commanded. (Ex. 39:43). |
| And God *blessed* the seventh day . . . (Gen. 2:3). | And Moses *blessed* them. (Ex. 39:43). |
| and made it *holy* . . . (Gen. 2:3). | . . . consecrate (the tabernacle and the altar) (Ex. 40:9-10). |

16. Weinfeld, "Sabbath, Temple and the Enthronement of the Lord," 503–4.

By recalling Genesis 1–2's depiction of the creation "sanctuary," the conclusion of Exodus not only suggests that the tabernacle is a micro-representation of that reality, but also that it provides a meaningful address of the problems that ensued within the creation "sanctuary": humanity's exile from God's presence and its refusal of divine instruction. Exodus, then, cannot be properly understood without its antecedent, Genesis.

Similarly with respect to the kingship pattern. The first two elements of the pattern in Exodus, the occasion for the conflict and battle, require Genesis' depiction of the occasion for and the conflict between the Creator and humanity to properly understand Exodus' role in the development of the pentateuchal solution to the fundamental narrative problem. Exodus provides two important links to such antecedents. First, the vocabulary describing Pharaoh's construction project recalls the building materials used in the Babel narrative, and Moses' salvation from the Nile in an ark (*ṭbh*, Ex. 2:3, 5) echoes the salvation of Noah and his family from the waters of chaos in the ark of God's design (and use in Gen. 6–9). Second, the final element of the pattern, the building, although designed and constructed in Exodus, evokes the creation narrative and its sanctuary symbolism, and is crucial in the subsequent books. In Leviticus, God speaks to Israel from the Tent of Meeting; in Numbers the Tent, located in the center of the military camp, defines all of life in the camp; Deuteronomy requires Israel to worship the Lord only at the place he chooses. In this way the four elements of the kingship pattern provide a conceptual coherence for the Pentateuch within this royal metaphor.

## The Meaning of Exodus, the Pentateuch, and Beyond

As a "royal inscription" of a Great King's victory over disorder in his empire, Exodus not only recalls the fundamental conflict between God and humanity and proclaims the Lord's victory over it at the Sea, but also witnesses to the construction of a concrete historical monument that proclaims his cosmic rule from a historically particular building: the tabernacle in the midst of Israel. As a coherent "royal inscription" Exodus must be heard as a whole, not from the perspective of one of its subplots, such as the victory at the Sea, or even that of the Sinai covenant legislation, but from the viewpoint of the cancellation of the narrative deficit: the "incarnation" of the triumphant King in the midst of his vassal people in the tabernacle. Neither victory at the Sea, Israel's submission to the covenant, nor the Lord's forgiveness of Israel's idolatry—individually or together—can express the full meaning of the Exodus narrative for they do not resolve the fundamental narrative problem which Exodus' plot structure develops: humanity's refusal of divine instruction and its consequent exile from God's presence. The resolution begins with the Lord's covenant and building instructions from Sinai, the glory cloud's indwelling of the tabernacle, and the subsequent instructions from the Tent of Meeting (Lev. 1:1). Similarly with the entire Pentateuch.

In its opening chapters Genesis depicts the Lord's earthly realm as suffering the intrusion of a pervasive disorder at the hands of the human community. The Lord moves against this disorder with judgments against Cain, the wickedness in the days of Noah, and the hubris of Babel. Unique redemptive action begins with Abram and his descendants. Like Abram, his descendants must separate themselves from the disorder of the nations which threaten this new community, especially when a new Pharaoh enslaves Jacob's descendants. After a decisive victory over Egypt the Lord moves into Israel's midst by means of the Tent of Meeting. This building is crucial for the rest of the Pentateuch because it discloses and develops the solution to the dual aspects of the fundamental problem: refusal of divine instruction and exile from God's presence. From the Tent God instructs his people and leads them toward the land promised to Abraham. Thus it, along with the other elements of the kingship pattern, provides the Pentateuch with conceptual coherence.

This building, also in its subsequent transformation as the temple on Mt. Zion in Jerusalem, is central to the Lord's administration of his rule over Israel (1 Kings 8:22–53). The nations will also stream to Jerusalem and from it the torah, the Lord's instruction, will flow to them (Isa. 2:2–4; cf. Isa. 19 with respect to Egypt and Assyria), for none of Adam's descendants can do without God's presence or his instruction. But when Israel defiles God's presence and refuses his instruction the glory cloud departs from the temple (Ezek. 8–10), God permits his servant Nebuchadnezzar (Jer. 25:9; 27:6; 43:10) to destroy Jerusalem and the temple, and removes Israel from his presence (2 Kings 24:3, 20; cf. 2 Kings 17:18, 20, 23). According to the New Testament the body of Christ becomes the temple of God's presence (John 1:14; 2:20–21; 1 Cor. 3:16) and earthly Jerusalem loses its centrality; the Lord's disciples move from Jerusalem to the ends of the earth (Acts 1:8) with the good news of the gospel, the torah of the Lord Jesus.[17] The church is now the place of God's presence and the locus of divine instruction. Thus the building project begun in creation and redemptively renewed in Exodus continues until a temple is no longer necessary and all the nations enjoy the presence of the Great King and walk by the light of the Lamb in the new Jerusalem (Rev. 21:22–27), the joy of the whole earth (Ps. 48:2).

---

17. For a fuller treatment of the temple and torah as fulfilled by Christ's ministry, see David E. Holwerda, "Jesus and the Temple: A Question of Essence," and "Jesus and the Law: A Question of Fulfillment," in his *Jesus & Israel: One Covenant or Two?* (Grand Rapids: Eerdmans, 1995), 59–83, 113–45.

# 4

# Genesis: The Journey
# Begins and Ends in Exile

**Summary**. God creates heaven, earth, and man: male and female, Adam and Eve. He blesses them. For failing to heed his instruction, God exiles them and their descendants from his presence and, after a universal flood, scatters them over the surface of the earth. God instructs Adam's descendant Abram to go to the land of Canaan, where God renames him Abraham and blesses him. Barren Sarah gives birth to Isaac, Abraham's only son. God blesses Isaac, who becomes the father of Esau and Jacob. Jacob deceives Isaac to get the firstborn's blessing. God blesses Jacob only after he honors his older brother Esau with a blessing. Jacob's sons deceive him into thinking Joseph is dead. After a universal famine, Joseph explains to his brothers that God sent him to Egypt and blessed him there to save the lives of many.

**Central narrative interest**. God blesses Abram so that through him all the nations may receive blessing (Gen. 12:1–3).

## The Narrative Problem of Genesis

The content and interplay of Genesis 1:1–2:3 and 2:4–4:26 define Genesis' narrative problem as the intrusion of disorder into the world, the result of Adam and Eve's failure to live according to divine instruction. By depicting the creation of all things as the result of the divinely spoken word, Genesis 1:1–2:3 describes reality from the viewpoint of the heavenly throne room. From his throne God's speaking distinguishes different aspects of the creation—water, earth, and the firmament—and makes all creatures, distinguishing them according to their kinds. God pronounces all this good, blesses it, and declares it fit for service by sanctifying the seventh day. Divine instruction is the origin of and necessary condition for creaturely life.

Beginning with Genesis 2:4 the narrative shifts to another point of view—the earth and the Garden of Eden—from which it describes relationships among God the Creator, the earth, and humanity. The first in a series of ten phrases—"this is the account of"—which structures the account of human activity upon the earth throughout the rest of Genesis (2:4; 5:1; 6:9; 10:1; 11:10; 11:27; 25:12; 25:19; 36:1; 37:2), not only highlights this shift in viewpoint, it also recalls the Lord's instruction for creation (1:1–2:3). Thus, when God instructs Adam "to work and take care of" the garden and not to eat from the tree of the knowledge of good and evil, he asks him to conform his person and life to the way God has structured the creation by his Word, including the subsequent instructions in the garden (2:15–17). When Adam and Eve fail so to conform their lives to divine instruction, God exiles them from his presence.

The Adam and Eve so exiled have a specific identity. If, as Wenham argues,[1] the opening chapters describe the creation and

---

1. Gordon J. Wenham, "Sanctuary Symbolism in the Garden of Eden Story," *Proceedings of the World Congress of Jewish Studies* 9 (1986): 19–25.

the garden as a sanctuary and Adam as a priest whose work is limited to and circumscribed by the creation-sanctuary, its structure, and the pertinent instructions, then Adam and Eve constitute a priestly pair. Biblical thought can only understand them as such: all who work in the near presence of God are priests and the obedience to which they are called is priestly conformity to divine instruction. Their failure to submit to God's instructions is nothing less than priestly defilement of the presence of God. The prominence of sanctuary and cultic instruction in Exodus through Numbers suggests that this reading is well within the bounds of what ancient Israel might have heard.

In sum, the problem which structures Genesis' narrative interest is the failure of Adam and Eve to live by divine instruction, their consequent defilement of that consecrated space where they lived in God's presence, and their expulsion from that consecrated space. Adam and Eve, and all their descendants are nothing less than a contaminated priestly community. Genesis begins to answer the question: How will, how can, a defiled priestly community return to God's presence—without which there is no true life—and enjoy that presence by priestly conformity to divine instruction? Genesis answers this question through a series of conflicts which reach a partial resolution in the story of Joseph, whose embalmed body remains in exile until Israel reaches the land.

## Plot in Genesis

Genesis is composed of four major conflicts, each of which sets the stage for a subsequent conflict. Together, and in their sequence, these conflicts develop the narrative problem and depict its partial resolution in the Joseph story.

## *The First Conflict: God, Adam, and the Nations (Gen. 2:4–11:26)*

The fundamental conflict, from which flow all subsequent human and cosmic conflicts depicted in the Pentateuch and the rest of Scripture, is that between God and Adam and Eve. Their disregard of the divine instructions leads them to hide from God, and God to pronounce the curse on the serpent, human life, and the earth. In the light of the subsequent biblical narrative their expulsion is both a necessary consequence of their sin—the unclean and the holy may not be in contact—and the occasion for God's redemptive activities—expulsion as "ritual death" provides space and time for an appropriate cleansing of the defiled human and creation community.

Life outside of God's presence is characterized by Cain's fratricide, Lamech's vengeance, and humanity's dedication to filling the earth with violence (cf. "to fill" in Gen. 1:28 and 6:11, 13). Human desecration turns God's approbation ("good" in Gen. 1:4, 10, 12, 18, 21, 25, 31) into the judgment "that every inclination of the thoughts of [man's] heart was only evil all the time" (Gen. 6:5). The immediate universal physical death held in abeyance at the time of Adam and Eve's sin becomes a reality when the Lord washes the impure from the face of the earth and subjects all creation to the waters of judgment in a universal flood. Like the expulsion from the garden, the flood was a necessary consequence of the desecration of God's presence; it also became the occasion for a divine act foundational for a new beginning: Noah, his family, and representatives of the animal kingdom are saved from cosmic destruction.

The flood depicts the inescapable consequences of the fundamental conflict between God and humanity. The ancients regarded the seas as a constant threat to life; they were also

## THE COVENANT WITH NOAH

The covenant with Noah, the first described as such in Genesis, displays features characteristic of the *royal grant* treaties of the ancient Near East.

The relationship between the Lord and Adam's descendants has deteriorated to the point that the Lord himself threatens the creation with a flood (Gen. 6:5–8).

In Genesis 9:8–17 God grants the righteous Noah (Gen. 6:9), his descendants, and all living things an earth free from the threat of flood waters. The rainbow, an empty war-bow pointed heavenward, constitutes a sign in the manner of a self-maledictory oath by which the Lord solemnizes the grant. The sign is available for all post-diluvian generations as a reminder of this *royal grant*.

Noah's descendants will show little of the righteousness for which God rewarded him. Nevertheless, for the sake of his commitment to one righteous man, God holds his judgment in abeyance. In the meantime, the future of the nations would be decided by God's dealing with another righteous man, Abraham.

mindful of the limits placed on the seas, whether below, on, or above the earth. Thus when the Lord removed these limits (Gen. 7:11; 8:2) he permitted disorder to overcome orderly living in the creation. Because the flood demonstrates the universal consequences of not heeding divine instruction, the Lord's regard of Noah, and the covenant he makes with him and all living things, is unexpected. For some unexplained reason Noah is found righteous and because of that receives divine instructions to build a vehicle that will withstand the waters of destruction.

Like the garden of Eden, the ark is constructed as a space for faithful living in the presence of God; unlike the garden, this space is continually threatened by chaos. Nevertheless, its divine design secures against all onslaught. Disorder threatens from without; God protects life within. Orderly living is possible only within that space created by divine instruction. Even so, neither the ark nor the covenant with all living creatures can resolve the fundamental human conflict between God and man. The post-flood earth, newly populated by the ark's inhabitants, is still beset by desecration: Ham sees his father's nakedness, and the nations gather to thwart God's purposes with a building project. Like Cain, Adam's descendants at Babel seek to establish their reputation by building a city whose technology would gain access to the heavens and so manage the disorder that threatens human life. Babel's attempt at managing the fundamental conflict and its consequences only reinforces the truth that all of Adam and Eve's descendants enjoy conflict with their Creator.

The confusion of tongues and the scattering of Adam's descendants has the apparent effect of bringing the people into conformity with the divine purpose to fill the earth (Gen. 1:28; 9:1). That is often how the scattering "over the face of the whole earth" of the Babel story is understood. Such a reading, however, ignores the peoples' filling the earth with violence (Gen. 6:11, 13) which led to the waters covering "all the surface of the earth" (Gen. 8:9). The scattering of Adam's descendants over the face of the earth should not, then, be read as the fulfillment of the divine purpose disclosed in Genesis 1:28 and 9:1, but as an extension of the chaos metaphor. Although the post-diluvial waters again flow within their limits and the Lord has promised never again so to destroy all living creatures (Gen. 8:21), the nations themselves now, like the waters of chaos, cover the earth. And, although they have received their assigned places (Deut.

32:8; Ps. 104:5–9; Job 38:8–11), the nations are a threat because they have transgressed the boundaries assigned to them. Like the great waters the nations threaten the orderliness of creation (cf. Jer. 51:55).[2] Within the depiction of the first conflict of Genesis, the flood and Babel symbolize the enduring chaos that threatens the good life: one expressing the consequences of the fundamental conflict on the level of human and non-human creation, the other on the level of human creatures.

Sin and its consequences do not abate in Genesis 2:4–11:26. Rather, disorder increases and becomes pervasive; Adam and Eve's descendants have no capacity for resolving the fundamental conflict between them and God. And, although humanity continues to experience the blessing of human fertility and regular times of harvest, the curse obtains, no one escapes. All who are born of Adam will die. God himself initiates action that will solve this unyielding predicament when he separates Abram from the chaos of the nations: "Leave your country, your people and your father's household and go to the land I will show you" (Gen. 12:1). Upon God's instruction Abram abandons all "natural" human ties, thereby reversing Adam's exile from his "natural" home in the presence of God. From now on his identity will no longer be rooted in his ancestors' home, its traditions, or the land of his birth, but in God's instructions and the land of promise.

Abram will be a stranger in this land, as will Isaac and Jacob. The land of God's promise is in every way unlike the land and

2. By synecdoche Babylon stands for the nations. Like the waters of chaos Babylon has swallowed Israel. In turn "the sea will rise over Babylon; its roaring waves will cover her," and "The Lord will destroy Babylon; he will silence her noisy din. Waves [of enemies] will rage like great waters; the roar of their voices will resound" (Jer. 51:42, 55). The phrase "great waters" refers to the threat of chaos. See H. G. May, "Some Cosmic Connotations of MAYIM RABBIM, 'Many Waters',ˮ *JBL* 74 (1955): 9–21.

soil in which the nations have cultivated their identities and response to God. Abram's resources for growth, wealth, and a name are completely unlike the nations' biological prowess and cultural means of production. Not the natural resources of the nations as Abram has come to know them in the land of his ancestors, but uniquely divine and redemptive resources begin to provide a resolution to the fundamental human conflict. God will bless Abram and his descendants, thereby working against the curse he himself had imposed and which obtains among the nations; God himself will bring Abram's descendants into his presence in the Promised Land. Nevertheless, when God separates Abram from his home, he does not abandon the nations. Rather, Abram and his descendants will be the instrument through whom God's blessing will come to the nations (Gen. 12:3b). They, too, will be rescued from relentless chaos. Abram's selection and the promise of progeny carries with it the seed of the second major narrative conflict, for Sarai is barren (Gen. 11:30).

### The Second Conflict: Barrenness (Gen. 11:27–25:18)

Although natural human reproduction and creative cultural technologies characterize the nations' activities in Genesis 2:4–11:26, these are not humanity's own "natural" resources. Rather, increase among the nations and their technological expertise are the regular and continuing result of God's blessing proclaimed in Genesis 1:28 and again in 9:7. The fundamental conflict between God and the nations has not undone these regular processes of creation;[3] they are part of the good which God bestows on all peoples.

3. Claus Westermann, *Blessing in the Bible and the Life of the Church*, trans. Keith Crim, OBT (Philadelphia: Fortress, 1978), 12–13.

It is all the more unusual, then, that this "natural" good does not carry over to Abram and Sarai. The divine promise of a new community embedded in God's speech of blessing to Abram conflicts with Sarai's barrenness: unlike the men in Genesis 5, 10, and 11, it is not said of Abram that "he became the father of . . . ," not even when Sarah does bear him a son (Gen. 21:1–7).[4] Abraham and Sarah cannot produce the promised future. Without a child there cannot be a great nation; without that nation Abraham's name will be only one among thousands of other men with hopes of a new future. The second major conflict in Genesis is that between God's promise of progeny and the human impossibility of creating that promised future.

The reader becomes aware of this conflict in Genesis 12:7 where God says to Abram, "To your offspring I will give this land," only a few verses after the narrative stated, "Now Sarai was barren; she had no children" (Gen. 11:30). As God's instruction to Abram to leave his ancestral home completely separated Abram from his cultural past, so now this promised future is cut off from the natural processes of community development. Even so, the narrative assures the reader that Sarai's barrenness will ultimately not stand in the way of the promised future: Genesis 12:7 suggests that there will be progeny; the means of its fulfillment, however, remains wholly unclear. What is already clear is that this promise is given in the presence of God who, in this appearing (r'h) to Abram, suggests the primacy of presence over the promise of land (r'h, 12:1). That is, God's appearing to Abram at this point is itself the gift that overshadows and characterizes Abram's wandering in the land.

4. Abraham's father Terah and brother Haran (11:27) are subjects of this verb in Gen. 11:27.

People and events external to and within the patriarchal family call attention to this conflict and play a variety of roles in the movement toward a satisfactory resolution of this conflict. Those external to the patriarchal family are Pharaoh and Abimelech, both of whom scheme to add Sarah to their household (Gen. 12, 20), and the women of the land of Canaan (Gen. 24 [cf. 26:34–35]). The episodes with Pharaoh and Abimelech depict possible obstacles to Sarah's offspring being Abraham's seed. Although Abraham worries about Sarah, it is the seed that is at stake: Who will be the father of the promised seed? In accordance with his word to Abram in 12:3a, the Lord watches over the promised future. Anticipating the wonders of Egypt, both royal houses suffer disease and plagues at the Lord's direction; and, ironically, the women of Abimelech's household are struck with barrenness. Only Abraham's intercession brings about healing for this household that, like the rest of the nations, would ordinarily be enjoying the continuous result of God's blessing. These two episodes indicate that neither Pharaoh nor Abimelech will shape Sarah's future. Neither Egypt nor Canaan will father Israel's promised future. But then, neither can nor will Abraham himself be the father of the promised seed. The Lord will be the Father of the "seed." The Creator and Redeemer himself will resolve Sarah's barrenness (Gen. 21:1b: "and the LORD did for Sarah what he had promised"). Isaac, and Israel, is born "not of natural descent, nor of human decision or a husband's will, but . . . of God" (John 1:13).

If Pharaoh and Abimelech may not father the "seed," neither may the mother of the promised future be anyone selected by Isaac. Thus Abraham charges his servant "not [to] get a wife for my son from the daughters of the Canaanites" (Gen. 24:3). Like Sarah before her, and Ruth later on (Ruth 2:11b), Isaac's wife must separate herself from her past, go to "the land," and join her future to that of Isaac. Like Sarah before her, Rebekah is also

## THE COVENANTS WITH ABRAHAM

God had promised Abram that he would become a great nation (Gen. 12:1–3), but Sarai was barren. In his childless state Abram presents this problem to the Lord, who repeats the promise of numerous offspring. Abram believes him and the Lord "counted it to him as righteousness" (Gen. 15:6).

With righteous Abram God makes a *royal grant* treaty by which God obligates himself with a self-maledictory oath—the blazing torch passing between the pieces of animals—to award Abram the Promised Land which his descendants would inherit. The land is given to Abram in perpetuity; his descendants may enjoy this gift to Abram, but not without emulating his righteousness.

This irrevocable grant of land to Abram is secure to all who imitate Abraham's faith (cf. Gal. 3:29).

When Sarai works with Hagar to bring about a family for Abram God intervenes and makes a second covenant with Abram (Gen. 17). In this *suzerain-vassal* treaty Abram and his descendants obligate themselves to the Lord by means of a self-maledictory oath implied in the sign of circumcision. A change of names—Abram becomes Abraham and Sarai, Sarah—lends significance to the occasion. God then promises Abraham a son to be born from Sarah, Isaac.

As with the Noahic covenant, it is significant that God binds himself to Abraham and his descendants with the royal grant. God's commitment forms the foundation for all the subsequent covenants with his people.

---

barren, and only the Lord's intervention enables her to become a mother in Israel (Gen. 25:21; cf. Ruth 4:13: "and the LORD enabled her to conceive"). Isaac's son Esau, however, marries "Judith the daughter of Beeri the Hittite, and also Basemath daughter of Elon the Hittite. They were a source of grief to Isaac and Rebekah" (Gen. 26:34–35; cf. 28:8–9; 36:2a).

People and events internal to the patriarchal family are Hagar and the sacrifice of Isaac. When Abram spoke of the conflict between the promise and Sarai's barrenness (Gen. 15:2–3), the Lord had assured him that he would have a son from his own body (Gen. 15:4). Abram believed God. But Sarai schemed her own solution to her barrenness: "The LORD has kept me from having children. Go, sleep with my maidservant; perhaps I can build a family through her" (Gen. 16:2). Although a son from Abram's own body, Ishmael is not the promised "seed." Because he is Abram's son, God will bless him and make him into a great nation (Gen. 17:20), but God's intervention among the nations through Abram will continue with Isaac, "whom Sarah will bear to you by this time next year" (Gen. 17:21; 18:13–14).

With Isaac's birth the conflict between barrenness and promise appears to have been resolved. But there is little joy in Abraham's household. When Ishmael's mockery causes distress, Abraham sends him and his mother into the desert, after which the Lord tests Abraham by requiring him to sacrifice "your only son Isaac, whom you love" (Gen. 22:2). Unlike Sarah, who sought to solve her barrenness in her own way, Abraham is prepared to await the Lord's provision, again. He submits to the Lord's terrible instruction and receives Isaac out of barrenness, for the second time; neither the barren womb nor the threatening tomb (cf. Prov. 30:16c, d, e) are obstacles to the promise. With this test of Isaac's sacrifice the second conflict is truly resolved. Now Abraham hears again the words spoken long ago: "I will surely bless you and make your descendants as numerous as the stars in the sky . . . and through your offspring all nations on earth will be blessed, because you obeyed me" (Gen. 22:17–18). Abraham, and the reader, now knows that God is the Father of Israel and the guardian of the promised "seed."

Through Isaac the fundamental conflict between the nations and God appears to be resolved. God blesses Isaac (Gen. 25:11), and Abimelech and Phicol, the commander of Abimelech's army, acknowledge Isaac as the blessed of God (Gen. 26:29). But how will the nations receive this blessing? Even as "your offspring" referred to Isaac when God spoke to Abraham in Genesis 12:7, now "your offspring" (Gen. 26:4) refers to Esau and Jacob. With that generation of Abraham's "seed," the narrative begins to develop the third major conflict.

## The Third Conflict: The Older and the Younger (Gen. 25:19–37:1)

The tension and conflicts between older and younger siblings is a theme that Genesis introduces with Cain and Abel, then carries through with Ishmael and Isaac, Esau and Jacob, and Leah and Rachel. These conflicts should be read against the background of the ancient custom of primogeniture, which rules that the oldest son has the rights of the firstborn, usually with respect to the nature and extent of the inheritance. Moreover, this right is not awarded by the father, but belongs to the son who "is the first sign of his father's strength," born of the favorite wife or not (Deut. 21:15–17). It is highly unusual, therefore, to find so many stories in Genesis where the younger receives the firstborn's share or is considered more important in some way. Even more unusual is that God, the Creator and Upholder of the universe, is depicted as overturning what among the nations was considered an unalterable custom. God prefers Abel and Isaac over Cain and Ishmael (Gen. 4:4; 17:20–21).

Keeping this in mind, we then understand why Jacob's purchase of the birthright from Esau and his deceit of Isaac to receive the blessing of the firstborn cause problems, and that on two levels. Conflict arises between Jacob and his family because he goes against accepted custom; and between him and God because Jacob himself overturns the order of things, rather than leaving it to God, who actually does prefer Jacob over Esau (Gen. 25:23). By doing it on his own, Jacob sows disorder within the patriarchal family and threatens the resolution of the fundamental conflict by means of the promised "seed."

That Jacob knew his purchase of the primogeniture was not righteous is evident from his later willingness to follow Rebekah's suggestion that he deceive Isaac to get the blessing of the firstborn. Although he escapes Esau's fury, Jacob cannot escape the consequences of his deceit. In Paddan Aram he receives justice at the hands of his uncle Laban. Jacob loves Rachel, the younger of Laban's daughters, and gets Laban's permission to marry her; on his wedding night Laban surprises him with the gift of the older sister, Leah. To Jacob's question, "Why have you deceived me?" Laban ironically replies, "It is not our custom here to give the younger daughter in marriage before the older one" (Gen. 29:26). The war between brothers turns into a contest between sisters.

After Rachel becomes Jacob's wife and discovers she is barren, she becomes jealous of her older and very fertile sister. Like Sarah before her, she then introduces a surrogate, Bilhah, so "that through her I too can build a family" (Gen. 30:3; cf. 16:2). When for a time Leah has no children, she also sends a surrogate to Jacob, Zilpah. The fertility fight waxes and wanes. At stake is the blessing of children; barrenness is a curse. God himself finally resolves the conflict when he opens Rachel's womb and she gives birth to Joseph.

The conflict between the brothers is resolved only when Jacob returns what he took from Esau illegitimately, the blessing. This he does when he sees Esau and tells him, "Please accept the present (*brkh* = blessing) that was brought to you, for God has been gracious to me and I have all I need" (Gen. 33:11). Only then does God bless Jacob and cleanse him from deceit by changing his name to Israel (Gen. 35:9). At that point God reaffirms the promise he had made to Jacob when he fled to Paddan Aram (Gen. 35:11–12; cf. 28:14). Jacob arrives home in time to see his father Isaac before his death.

Although the third conflict is resolved by Jacob's return of the birthright, he soon reaps the harvest of deceit within his own family. Because Joseph is Rachel's son, Jacob loves him more than the older brothers and gives him a richly ornamented robe, thereby doing what Deuteronomy 21:15–17 prohibits. Thus Jacob precipitates the fourth major conflict.

### The Fourth Conflict: Joseph ben Abraham and His Brothers (Gen. 37:2–50:26)

Like Esau, and Cain before him, Joseph's older siblings hate their younger brother. When Joseph recounts to them his dreams about the family's subservience to him, murder slithers up to the door (Gen. 37:20; cf. 4:7–8). The murderous intent that characterized the nations early in Genesis (i.e., Cain and his descendant Lamech), and that entered the patriarchal community through Jacob's deceit of Isaac and Esau, now comes to fruition among Jacob's "seed." The fourth conflict not only depicts the consequences of Jacob's deceit in his own family, but also shows, by echoing the Cain and Abel story, that the Abraham community, chosen by God to be a solution to the nations, is itself contaminated with the problem that led to God's separating Abraham

73

from the nations. This conflict, then, evokes an element of the first with the further complication that the brothers' hatred endangers the journey to the land that Abraham began with God. Any impediment to this journey jeopardizes God's blessing of the nations. Thus, the fourth conflict gathers within itself all the major issues presented by the first three: the incapacity of the nations to solve their problem and Abraham's election; the barrenness of Sarah and God's provision of the chosen "seed"; mismanagement of the blessing by the chosen "seed."

The brothers' hatred endangers the journey to the land because their action removes Joseph (and ultimately the whole family) from Canaan by selling him into exile in Egypt. Jacob himself was forced into exile after he got Esau to sell him the birthright. After Jacob returned to the land, his sons Simeon and Levi endanger the community with their shameful actions in Shechem (Gen. 34:30). In Genesis 37 the brothers' actions in the land force Joseph into Egyptian slavery. The narrative then briefly shifts to the story of Judah's unrighteous actions with his daughter-in-law, Tamar, in the land. Abraham's descendants live in the Promised Land, but there Jacob deceived Isaac and provoked Esau's fury, there Simeon and Levi endangered Abraham's offspring, there the brothers send Joseph to "death" by expelling him from the family, and there Judah—the one, as the reader knows, from whom will come Israel's salvation—commits unrighteous acts.

The land of promise appears to be anything but a place of blessing and the patriarchal family anything but good. Jacob and his sons themselves endanger the journey by their deceit and murderous intent. Like Joseph, they will be exiled, as was father Abram shortly after he arrived in the land (12:10–20). Like father, like son. In the remainder of Genesis the action shifts from the Promised Land to Egypt.

Joseph enjoys God's favor in Egypt, but his situation deteriorates because of the incident with Potiphar's wife and he is imprisoned. But, even as God responded to Cain's murderous intent and Jacob's deceit (Gen. 4:6–7; 28:14–15), so now in Egypt the Lord deals with Joseph ("The LORD was with Joseph," 39:2, 3, 21, 23) with the result that Potiphar's house is blessed (39:5). Joseph is also successful in prison. His interpretation of Pharaoh's dreams brings him to high office in Egypt where he prepares Egypt for seven years of famine. He is so successful and skilled that "all the countries came to Egypt to buy grain from Joseph, because the famine was severe in all the world" (Gen. 41:57). Joseph, son of Abraham, "exiled" from the land by his brothers' hatred and murderous intent, keeps universal disorder at bay by his wise administration of Egypt. Although Abraham's "seed" interrupted the journey to the land in various ways, they could not prevent God's blessing from coming to the nations. The nations survive the chaos of the famine by the righteous acts of Joseph, the "seed" of Abraham. Joseph's administration of the "Food for the World" program also impels the narrative toward its solution of the murderous intent between the brothers: the famine forces them to deal with Joseph.

When they meet, Joseph forces his brothers to acknowledge the truth about their relationship with their youngest sibling (Gen. 42:13, 15, 20, 32). This not only evokes the memory of their treatment of the younger brother they now believe to be dead, but also evokes the theme of the younger and older in the Jacob-Esau and Cain-Abel stories. In Joseph's self-disclosure to his brothers and his explanation of God's purposes in their selling him into Egypt, the narrative solves the conflict between Joseph and his brothers, and discloses an important contrast with the Cain-Abel story. As a powerful governor, Joseph could have imprisoned them as Pharaoh did with the baker, but he instead returns good for ill.

He also places their murderous intent within a wholly unexpected framework: "it was to save lives that God sent me ahead of you . . . so it was not you who sent me here, but God" (Gen. 45:5, 8). Cain had killed his brother Abel; Joseph's brothers did not kill him—not because they were more righteous than Cain, but because God intended to use Joseph's righteous actions for the greater good. Joseph's acknowledgment of God's action in his misery and rise to power in Egypt reconciles the older and the younger.

Although the conflict between the brothers has been resolved, there remains the problem of the family's moving to Egypt. Joseph's exile to Egypt has saved Abraham's "seed" and brought the blessing of life to the nations. But should Jacob and the rest of the family also move to Egypt? As before, when Jacob fled to Paddan Aram, so now God encourages him: "Do not be afraid to go down to Egypt, for I will make you a great nation there. I will go down to Egypt with you, and I will surely bring you back again" (Gen. 46:3–4; 28:13–15). So the bearer of the promise goes to Egypt, and it, not Canaan, becomes the place of Israel's spectacular growth. Egypt will also bestow its riches on God's people: Abram receives the firstfruit of Egypt (Gen. 12:16), his descendants its spoils (Gen. 47:6, 11, 27; cf. Ex. 1:7; 12:35–36).

Some time after he moves to Egypt, Jacob blesses his children and dies. His children take him back to the Promised Land to be buried in Machpelah like Abraham, Sarah, and Isaac before him. As the Lord had told him, Jacob has returned to the land, there to await a greater fulfillment of the promise. When Joseph's brothers beg Joseph's forgiveness, he reminds them of God's ways and reassures them. Before Joseph dies, his brothers promise that, when God brings the family to the Promised Land, they will take his remains along. Joseph will await that day in Egypt.

In sum, the resolution of the conflict between the brothers also brings to closure certain elements of the fundamental conflict as depicted in Genesis 4–11. But this solution, especially the move to Egypt, carries with it elements of the conflict between Israel and Pharaoh, a conflict taken up in Exodus.

## The Structures of Genesis

Genesis tells its story by focusing on particular people: Adam, Noah, Abram, Isaac, Jacob, and Joseph; but it does not begin with any of these. Before the reader gets any sense of who these people are or what they do, the narrative depicts God's creation of all things and creatures, and his declaration that all of it is very good (1:1–2:3). Within this creation God blesses the man and the woman and gives them a unique task (1:28; cf. 2:15).

Beginning with Genesis 2:4 the phrase "This is the account of . . ." (Gen. 2:4; 5:1; 6:9; 10:1; 11:10, 27; 25:12, 19; 36:1; 37:2)[5] alternatively introduces narrative and genealogical texts. The narratives focus on particular people and situations; the genealogies link one epoch to another (e.g., 5:1 links Adam to Noah), or provide a brief genealogical account of someone who then disappears from the narrative (Ishmael in 25:12). In their structuring of Genesis these accounts variously focus the reader on the succeeding generations of Adam and Eve's descendants, blessing and curse, order and disorder.

### *From One Generation to the Next: The Toledoth*

Beginning with Genesis 2:4 the narrative devotes ten sections to telling the story of human response to God within his creation. Each section begins with the phrase "This is the account of . . ." as in Genesis 2:4: "This is the *account* of the

---

5. The "account" of Esau in 36:9 is a further expansion of the "account" of 36:1.

heavens and the earth when they were created." "Account," a translation of the Hebrew *toledoth*, is a nominal form of the verb "to bear, to give birth," which stands for that which was produced or generated. Thus, in the phrase "the account of the heavens and the earth," the word "account" refers to the end result, or what became of the heavens and the earth, and the phrase "of the heavens and the earth," refers to the starting point.[6] Thus, the section beginning in 2:4 is not the story of heaven and earth, but what happened with the creation as a result of Adam and Eve's response to God. The literary function of these opening formulas is to recall the antecedent narrative as the basis from which the narrative recounts what happened subsequently.

These *toledoth* formulas shape the entire Genesis narrative. By linking the ongoing story to its antecedents these ten accounts describe what happened to the good creation under human direction, each one anchored in a particular human response to God. What begins well (2:4, see "good" in 1:1–2:3) in God's good presence, ends with a divine curse and human vengeance (3:17; 4:23–24); the story of Adam (5:1–2) begins with God's blessing and ends with human perversion and God's repenting of having created man (6:1–7); the story of Noah begins with a righteous man (6:9) and ends with a curse on Canaan (9:25); the sons of Noah story (10:1) ends with the arrogance of Babel (11:1–9); and the story of Shem (11:10) ends with a reference to Abraham as the son of Terah (11:26). Similarly in 11:27; 25:12, 19; 36:1; and 37:2. In sum, the ten accounts of Genesis 2:4–50:26 describe what happened to and in the orderly creation,

6. David Carr, "Βίβλος γενέσεος Revisited: A Synchronic Analysis of Patterns in Genesis as Part of the Torah," *ZAW* 110 (1998): 159–72, 327–47; Marten H. Woudstra, "The *Toledoth* of the Book of Genesis and their Redemptive-Historical Significance," *CTJ* 5 no. 2 (1970): 184–89.

depicted in Genesis 1:1–2:3, under the direction of Adam, Eve, and their descendants.

A closer examination of the narrative development reveals a shift from a universal to a particular point of view. The first five accounts (2:4–11:26) treat the descendants of Adam and Eve, the nations. No nation receives favorable treatment; they all move away from God; all are affected by the flood; and all are scattered from Babel. Except for Noah, no one is righteous; all the nations are subjected to the curse. With the Terah account (11:27) the narrative moves to the particular: God instructs Abram to separate himself from his ancestral home and go to the land, i.e., the Promised Land. After this the accounts focus on Abram and his descendants, but among these only Isaac, Jacob, and Joseph receive extended attention. Others are only briefly mentioned in relation to the major characters and short genealogical accounts (Abraham's other sons, 25:1–4; Ishmael, 25:12–18; Esau, 36:1–37:1). At Genesis 11:27, then, the narrative interest of Genesis, having begun with a universal perspective, shifts to God's particular blessing of one family and its divinely appointed role among the nations. This focus controls the narrative interest to the end of Genesis, throughout the rest of the Old Testament, and into the New Testament (Matt. 1:1, 18; Gal. 3:29).

The shift to the particular after 11:27 does not imply a rejection of the nations, only that God's blessing of the nations will now, in some sense not yet clear to the audience, be received through Abram. The birth of descendants throughout the generations of Adam and Eve points to God's abiding interest in the nations. Only God's blessing (1:28) enables Adam and Eve's descendants to enjoy the blessing of fertility: at home with children, in culture with the development of music and other arts, including the building of cities. Thus the human community enjoys enormous gifts and powers which remain theirs to exercise, even though God has cursed the earth, made human work difficult, and expelled man from his presence.[7]

The account formulas themselves suggest this continuity by repeatedly using the nominal form of the verb "to bear; to give birth"; the verb also regularly appears in the genealogies of Genesis (chaps. 5, 10, 11, 25, 36). Nevertheless, even though human fertility and cultural activity continue unabated, these cannot solve the fundamental problem. At Babel the Lord frustrates Adam's descendants' attempts to make a name for themselves with their cultural resources (11:1–9).[8] Despite receiving enormous cultural powers from God, human history as depicted in Genesis is a story of increasing conflict with God. Babel becomes a shameful monument to humanity's attempt to generate its own secure existence. "In Adam" humanity cannot overcome the Lord's curse (3:14, 17; 4:11; 5:29; 9:25; Rom. 5:12).

"In Abram" the curse is also a problem, for he also shares the identity of the nations of whom Adam is the father. For that reason the shift to the particular in the sixth account is accompanied by a brief reference to Sarah's barrenness (11:30). Unlike the fertile nations, Abram and Sarai have no power to contribute to the community of nations; they are completely dependent upon the God who overwhelms Abram with a symphony of promises (12:1–3), including a word of blessing that will shape the subsequent accounts of Abram and his seed.[9]

7. On the constancy of blessing as distinguished from events of deliverance, see Westermann, *Blessing in the Bible and the Life of the Church*.

8. The narrative here uses the phrase "the descendants of Adam," thereby linking the problems of this generation to their forebear.

9. "Yahweh is the subject of the first verb at the beginning of the first statement and thus the subject of the entire subsequent sacred history." Gerhard von Rad, *Genesis: A Commentary* (London: SCM Press, 1961), 159.

In the first five accounts Genesis moves from a refusal of divine instruction and the consequence of expulsion from the presence of God to a scattering throughout the world. Beginning with the sixth account the narrative moves from an instruction to abandon the scattered nations and travel to the Promised Land, to a place of "exile" among the nations, far from the Promised Land. Although Joseph is exiled in Egypt, this descendant of Adam "in Abraham" has received a promise, has experienced its firstfruits in Egypt, and waits in eager expectation for its greater fulfillment (50:24–25; cf. Rom. 8:19). According to Genesis, God has brought the descendants of Abraham closer to his presence than those who remain under the curse "in Adam." He has done so by partially fulfilling the blessing he promised to Abraham.

- *1:1–2:3: God creates the heavens and the earth*
- *2:4–50:26: What became of them among Adam and Eve's descendants?*
  2:4–11:26—among the nations (refusal of instruction and expulsion from presence)
    2:4—the account of the heavens and the earth
    5:1—the account of Adam
    6:9—the account of Noah
    10:1—the account of Shem, Ham, and Japheth
    11:10—the account of Shem
  11:27–50:26—among Abraham and his seed (submission to instruction and moving toward the presence of God)
    11:27—the account of Terah
    25:12—the account of Ishmael
    25:19—the account of Isaac
    36:1—the account of Esau
    37:2—the account of Jacob

## Curse and Blessing in Genesis

After the fall, Adam, Noah, and their descendants experience God's blessing (1:28; 9:1, 7), but always in the shadow of the curse (3:14, 17; 4:11; 5:29; 9:25), which has the effect of excluding the affected person from the security, justice, and successes of the community whose blessings he had earlier enjoyed.[10] Thus the descendants of Adam wander restlessly (4:12), wantonly fill the earth with violence (6:11, 13, cf. 1:28), and seek the security of a city built for their own reputation (11:1–9). In spite of the continuing blessing evidenced by enormous human growth in the first five "accounts," the effect of the curse makes itself felt. Outside of God's presence, death is a regular part of the human experience. It is inescapable for all of Adam's descendants, except for Abram and Sarai and their descendants (1 Cor. 15:45–49; Gal. 3:14).

If Babel memorializes humanity's attempt to secure its own existence, then Sarai's barrenness, emblematic of the future that awaits all nations, continually reminds Israel that her life, well-being, and reputation are totally dependent upon God. The theme of "barrenness," whether associated with human infertility (Rebekah [25:21], Rachel [29:31]) or famine (12:10; 41:56–57), does not vanish from the narrative after God begins dealing with Abram. Rather, it becomes the occasion for demonstrating the true source of fertility, i.e., God's blessing, and for defining the only place where a blessed future is secure, i.e., "in Abram" (41:56–57; and Ex. 16; Num. 11; Deut. 7:12–14; 11:13–17).

God's promises to Abram repeat the verb "to bless" five times; equal to the number of times that "to curse" (heb. 'rr) occurs in Genesis 3:1–11:26. In addition, God makes these

10. 'rr, *TDNT*, Vol. 1, 408–9.

promises to Abram: "you" in 12:2–3 is second person singular. This suggests that the effect of the curse will be affected by blessing Abram. God himself will accomplish this; he is the subject of the main verbs in 12:2–3, beginning with separating Abram from the culture of Babel. Furthermore, a break in this sequence at 12:3b—"should there be one who regards you with contempt I will curse him"—underscores the primacy of God's purpose to bless.[11] God pronounced the curse upon Adam and his descendants—the nations—for their refusal of his instruction. Now, although it is God's intention to bless Abram, and through him the nations, God so identifies this purpose with Abram that he will curse anyone who treats Abram lightly. God will not allow Abram to suffer the opposition he himself receives in Genesis 3:1–11:26, not from outside (Pharaoh and Abimelech, 12:10–20; 20:1–18) nor from inside (27:41; 37:19–20) Abram's family. The curse which brings forth barrenness will be replaced by blessing: God will make Abram into a great nation.

With Abram God only begins to undo the curse; the effects of the curse continue among him and his seed. Sarah's struggle to realize the blessing by her own ingenuity has its parallel in Jacob's deceit of Isaac and in Jacob's sons' deceit of their father when they sell Joseph into slavery. And death triumphs over everyone. Nevertheless, God's blessing obtains: he miraculously gives Isaac life, twice; he tricks Jacob into admitting he has stolen the blessing from Esau; and he guides Joseph to a regal position from which he saves Abraham's seed from death and administers the blessing of food to all the peoples of the earth. Thus, when they arrive in Egypt, Abram's descendants are seventy (46:27). Even Ishmael and Esau are blessed with many descendants (25:12–18;

11. Translation by Patrick D. Miller, "Syntax and Theology in Genesis XII 3a," *VT* 34 (1984): 474.

36:37). "In Abram" there is blessing for his descendants, and the nations. "In Abram" the curse of barrenness becomes the blessing of fertility.

If we go back to the beginning of the account of Terah (11:27) and ask: What became of Terah? we may confidently answer: What began in a culture of disobedience and barrenness has ended with fruitfulness, blessing, and a confident expectation of a blessed future in the land of promise. After God instructs Abram, the narrative relates what God begins to do through Abram (11:27–25:10), develops with Jacob (25:19–35:29), and completes with Joseph (37:2–50:26). From the point of view of curse and blessing the narrative moves from Adam and Eve's descendants outside of the garden to Abraham and Sarah's descendants in Egypt. Although they have not yet arrived in the presence of God, he has been with them all the way from Ur and Haran to Egypt.

| 1:1–2:3 | **God blesses the creation** | |
|---|---|---|
| 2:4–11:26 | **From blessing to curse in Adam: outside the garden** | |
| | 2:4–4:26 | From blessing to curse in Adam |
| | 5:1–6:8 | From blessing in Adam to wickedness |
| | 6:9–9:29 | From judgment to blessing |
| | 10:1–11:9 | Blessing by birth upon the sons of Noah to scattering |
| | 11:10–26 | Blessing by birth through Shem |

| 11:27–50:26 | **From curse to blessing in Abram: toward the land** |
|---|---|
| 11:27–25:11 | God blesses Abram and his seed |
| 25:12–18 | God blesses Ishmael |
| 25:19–35:29 | God removes barrenness from Abram's family: Jacob and Esau |
| 36:1–37:2 | God blesses Esau |
| 37:2–50:26 | God blesses the nations "in Abram": Joseph |

Although "exiled" in Egypt, Joseph has experienced the first-fruits of God's blessing of Abraham's seed and the nations in Egypt, for he has seen his children's children, and died blessed (50:23; Ps. 128:6). "In Abram" God has rescued these descendants of Adam from the curse and blessed them. He has done so by confronting the tumult of the nations "in Abram."

### From Order to Disorder: Death

The ancient world feared nothing so much as the intrusion of disorder. For that reason Genesis 1:1–2:3 is nothing but good news in that world. Orderliness characterizes the creation because God's commands are obeyed: "Let there be . . . and it was so"; creatures receive their places: celestial bodies in the heavens and the land, the sea, and creatures of the air in their respective places; and orderly reproduction of plant and animal life is secured: "after their own kinds" (Gen. 1:11, 12, 21, 24). No other "deities" of the air, land, or sea make mischief; indeed, the earth is filled with nothing but ordinary creatures. Humanity, uniquely identified as God's image-bearer, also receives a blessing to be fruitful (1:28; cf. 2:15–17) and take care of the earth and its creatures. God declared all of this "very good" (1:31), and then "rested from all the work of creating he had done" (2:3). The creation was complete, bursting with life, it lacked nothing necessary for an orderly and careful development under human direction. Above all, there was no threat; water was merely water, flowing in its proper places.

Everyone knows, however, that life in the creation as we experience it has its problems. Where does that trouble come from? Not from the fiber of creation itself, for it has all it needs to be what the Creator wants it to be. Disorder will enter if humanity fails to manage the creation in God's presence according to his will; humanity will then surely die (2:15–17). The instruction does not bring disorder; it sets forth the conditions for good orderly living. After receiving that instruction Adam rejoices in Eve.

The narrative shifts abruptly with a play on the word "naked," thereby linking the narrative circumstances of Adam and Eve's orderly lives to the "crafty"[12] serpent and the temptation scene. In this scene the serpent contends that death is not a problem (3:4) and successfully argues that Eve may dispute the divinely assigned places of work, aspire to move beyond creaturely limits, and so gain full knowledge. By submitting to the serpent's temptation, Eve and Adam open the door to death. Like flood waters overrunning a fertile field, so disorder in the form of death

---

12. The underlying Hebrew consonants for both words are '*rwm*. For brief studies on "sea" and "serpent" see the entries in Karel Van Der Toorn, et al., *Dictionary of Deities and Demons in the Bible*, 2nd rev. ed. (Leiden: Brill; Grand Rapids: Eerdmans, 1999). For iconographic depictions of the chaos-monster, the dragon, and its relationship to the sea, see Othmar Keel, *The Symbolism of the Biblical World: Ancient Near Eastern Iconography and the Book of Psalms*, trans. Timothy J. Hallett (New York: Seabury, 1978), 49–56.

will swallow the good. God exiles Adam and Eve. They are the first of the living dead: outside of God's presence there is no life. Consequently death becomes the great enemy; it will undermine the blessing of fertility and defile all human culture.

Where the introduction to Genesis depicted a creation bursting with life, the first five toledoth describe one bristling with death. Cain kills Abel; the dark refrain "and then he died" marks all Adam's descendants; the once-good waters, now loosed to destroy, bring the death of all life. But death did not enter the ark. Though Noah eventually dies, his descendants by Shem enjoy life and multiply. None of these descendants die until the sixth toledoth: Haran and Terah (11:28, 32). And Sarah is barren. Abram cannot become a father. That he does is a sign of God's working against the power of death.

Death also defiles the moral realm. A drama of increasing wickedness—Adam and Eve's desire to be like God, their son's fratricide, Lamech's vengeful attitude, and the defiling coupling of the sons of God and daughters of men—leads to God's seeing "how great man's wickedness on the earth had become, and that every inclination of the thoughts of his heart was only evil all the time" (6:5). And so the great waters swallowed up life. God pronounces the blessing (9:1, 7) in a cleansed though still troubled (9:2) creation, but Adam's descendants (11:5) at Babel repeated their ancestors attempt to be like God. There is no human life that is not fundamentally touched by disorder.

The next five toledoth describe the hope of new life and fertility among the descendants of Abram, also defiled by death. Abraham and Sarah wait years for the promised son, during which time the promised newness is repeatedly threatened: Sarah's womb is endangered by Pharaoh (12:17) and Abimelech (20:3–7; cf. 26:10), and the Lord himself takes Abraham to the brink of killing the promised one (22:10–11). Subsequently,

Jacob opens the door to death by his scheming against Isaac and Esau. Deceit is repaid by a deceit that initiates the fertility wars. In Canaan, Simeon and Levi serve death in the name of family honor (34:1–31). Death lies at the door, but God blesses his chosen, keeping death at bay, and so the family grows. Jacob's deceit has sown deeply: his sons threaten Joseph with death and claim that he has died. But God was with Joseph, keeping death at bay so that Jacob's family and all the families of the earth might cheat death at the hand of a universal famine. God's word to Abraham is true: blessing overcomes barrenness and death.

At the end of Genesis death overwhelms the righteous one appointed to save the nations from disaster; he saved others but could not save himself. Death has not triumphed, but its threat does not abate. All of Abraham's descendants will die. But they die in hope: Abraham, Sarah, Isaac, and Jacob enjoy the firstfruits of their inheritance in the grave of Machpelah. Joseph, embalmed in Egypt, awaits the day when he too will receive his rest (Josh. 24:32; Heb. 4). By the end of Genesis we know that death will have no victory. But the journey to the complete restoration of God's good order will require waiting and patience. We can see this expressed in the following outline:

| | |
|---|---|
| **1:1–2:3** | **God creates the heavens and the earth: very good** |
| **2:4–11:26** | **From life to death and increasing disorder** |
| **11:27–50:26** | **From death to life and increasing order** |
| | 11:27–37:1     Among the descendants of Abraham |
| | 37:2–50:26     Among all the descendants of Adam |

The occasion for disorder is of course the temptation of the serpent. If his influence appears rather benign in Genesis, Exodus reveals his malevolent intent in the person of Pharaoh, whose persona is the ancient dragon monster (*tnyn*, Ex. 7:8–13). But at the Sea the swallower himself is swallowed (Ex. 15:12; cf. 7:12). Although the wrong seems oft so strong, God is the Ruler yet.

## Waiting for the Land: Death Be Not Proud

Genesis opens with God's exiling humanity from his presence for its failure to abide by the divine instruction; so death entered the world. Although physical death was held in abeyance for Adam and Eve, the expulsion from God's presence for disobedience provides a foretaste of this death: existence under the curse.

Because death enters the world in Genesis 3, Adam's descendants all die (Gen. 5:1–27). Death still exercises its power in Genesis 49–50, for Abraham's descendants cannot escape the consequences of Adam's disobedience. Nevertheless, as Genesis concludes, Jacob and Joseph do not die as those who have no hope, for they have a place of rest. Jacob's sons bury him in the burial plot Abraham bought from Ephron, the cave at Machpelah (Gen. 23; 50:13). When Joseph dies in Egypt, however, he is embalmed, then to await God's time for his transport to the land God promised to Abraham, Isaac, and Jacob (Gen. 50:24–26; cf. Josh. 24:32).

Although a universal threat, at the end of Genesis the curse of death has been hemmed in by God's promised blessing to Abraham: he opened the barren wombs of Sarah, Rebekah, and Rachel; through Joseph God saved the nations from deadly famine. And, although they are in Egypt, the Promised Land is closer to becoming a reality: Machpelah is the firstfruits of their "possession" (*'ḥzh*). But they receive it only in death.

The word "site" or "plot" in the phrase "burial site" (*'ḥzt qbr*) indicates a holding in trust[13] not a permanent inheritance. This would seem to have little significance, for the dead hold nothing. But in the light of Genesis 17:8, where the land is promised as an "everlasting possession" (*'ḥzt 'wlm*), it becomes clear that the land itself, though the goal for Abraham and his descendants, will only be held in trust, and that in perpetuity. It never is truly theirs; they will always be the Lord's tenants, as indicated by Abraham's status as an alien (Gen. 23:4, *gr wtwšb*) and the land as "the land of your alienness" (Gen. 17:8, *'rṣ mgryk*).

Genesis ends with death hemmed in, but still a certainty; with the land still only a distant reality, yet gained in death. Hemmed-in death and the Promised Land are the twin elements of the eschatology of Genesis. By their dying the patriarchs suffer the punishment of all Adam's descendants; but their grave is in the land of promise so that, unlike Adam's other descendants, they enjoy the firstfruits of God's promise, not only in life—the gift of descendants and prosperity—but also in death, the land itself. Death will continue to exercise its power among the descendants of Abraham: the little ones swallowed by the waters of death in Egypt; disobedient priests (Lev. 10); Israel in the desert (Num. 13–14); its arrogant leaders Korah, Dathan, Abiram, and their followers (Num. 16). But even death is put on notice when in Exodus proud Egypt is swallowed (Ex. 7:13; 15:12) and God's people escape its grasp on dry ground. Thus the song at the Sea praises the Lord not only for his defeat of the enemy, but also for establishing his

13. Jacob Milgrom, "Sweet Land and Liberty," *Bible Review* 9 (August 1993): 8; and see his *Leviticus 17–22*, AB (New York: Doubleday, 2000): 1326, 1328.

people in the land of their inheritance (Ex. 15:17). Later, when God's people await the punishment for their sin at the hand of nations who, like death, would swallow them to end their future, Isaiah expands the vision of death's limited power and time: "On this mountain he will destroy the shroud that enfolds all peoples, the sheet that covers all nations; he will swallow up death forever. The Sovereign Lord will wipe away the tears from all faces; he will remove the disgrace of his people from all the earth" (Isa. 25:7–8), and when that happens all Israel's exiles "will come and worship the Lord on the holy mountain in Jerusalem" (Isa. 27:13).

Hemmed-in death and the land come into view again with the ministry of Jesus, who reveals that a particular mountain or city is no longer important (John 4:21). What is crucial is that Christ dwell in the midst of those who believe in him and worship in Spirit and truth. That indwelling blesses work that is not in vain (1 Cor. 15:58), for "death has been swallowed up in victory" (1 Cor. 15:54). Even so, the dead in Christ, like the patriarchs and Joseph, await the time of his coming; like them they are buried in a grave that is held in trust for them, not by Abraham's 400 shekels of silver, but by the precious blood of Christ (1 Peter 1:18–19), "the first fruits of those who have fallen asleep" (1 Cor. 15:20).

# 5

## Exodus: From Pharaoh's Store Cities to the Lord's Throne Room

**Summary**. When Jacob's descendants become numerous in Egypt, Pharaoh fears them. He enslaves them to build his cities, but God raises up Moses to deliver them that they may serve him. Ten plagues upon Egypt force Pharaoh to let Israel go to serve God. The Egyptian army pursues the Israelites but drowns in the sea God opened for Israel's escape. In the desert Israel complains about water and food; God supplies their needs. At Mt. Sinai God reveals himself in thunder and fire and offers Israel a covenant which the people accept, and Moses instructs them in the terms of the covenant. God then reveals to Moses his design for a tabernacle. Israel will build it so God can dwell among them. But Israel builds a golden calf and provokes God to anger. Moses intercedes for Israel but many die for their rebellion. God forgives his people and renews the covenant. Then Israel volunteers offerings for the tabernacle, they build its various parts, Moses assembles it, and the glory cloud fills the tabernacle.

**Central narrative interest.** Through Moses, God brings Abraham's descendants out of Egypt and leads them to his presence at Sinai, where they meet with the God who will dwell among them (Ex. 29:42–46).

## Connection with Antecedent Narrative

Exodus begins with a brief review of Jacob's entry into Egypt, noting that Joseph preceded the family, and that Joseph and his generation have died. In contrast with this death notice, Exodus goes on to describe the enormous growth of these descendants of Abraham in language that recalls the familiar words of God's declaration of blessing at the time of creation, after the flood, and to the patriarchs repeatedly: "but the Israelites were fruitful and multiplied greatly and became exceedingly numerous, so that the land was filled with them" (Ex. 1:7; cf. Gen. 1:28; 9:1, 7; 17:2, 20; 22:17; 26:4, 24; 35:11; 47:27; 48:4). By recalling these blessings in reference to Jacob's descendants, the narrator makes this amazing statement about Israel: What God had intended for all Adam's descendants from the beginning, and declared to be his will again after the flood, has become a reality among Abraham's descendants in the land of Egypt.[1] This blessing also provides the occasion for Pharaoh's violent response and subsequently the definition of the narrative problem of Exodus.

1. But not yet over the whole earth. The Hebrew for "land" also means "earth." Its primary meaning in Ex. 1:7 is "land," but, especially in the context of the familiar words of the blessing of Gen. 1:28, the reader also is reminded of the whole earth. That is God's ultimate purpose. Similarly God's promise of land to Abraham (Gen. 12:1), initially meaning the Promised Land, is taken by Paul as "cosmos" (Rom. 4:13).

## Narrative Problem and Plot

Exodus is composed of three major conflicts, each of which sets the stage for a subsequent conflict. Together, and in their sequence, these conflicts take the reader from the narrative problem defined in Exodus 1–2 to its resolution as depicted in Exodus 39–40.

### *The Narrative Problem of Exodus*

Pharaoh's enslavement of Israel to the forced building of his store cities (Ex. 1:8–14; 5:1–23) constitutes the narrative problem, or deficit, of Exodus. Ancient imperial building programs, commonly executed with slave labor, were part of the royal propaganda machine: great temples, cities, and palaces expressed the wealth and power of the ruler. Thus, when Pharaoh forces Israel to build Pithom and Rameses, they glorify his reign, and not the reign of the God whose servants they are as descendants of Abraham. This enslavement prompts the question, "Whom will Israel serve?" or, "Who will be Israel's master: Pharaoh or God?"[2] By Exodus 15:21 Israel is free from Pharaoh, but we still do not have an answer to the question. Israel's relationship to God is far from clear, and the desert narrative suggests that Israel is barely dedicated to God's interests. What will happen to Israel now that she has left Egypt? What will Israel do to glorify the reign of her God? Exodus answers these and other questions, and ends with an extensive account of another building program.

2. On the role of Exodus 1–2 and the question which the Exodus narrative answers, see Charles Isbell, "Exodus 1–2 in the context of Exodus 1–14: Story Lines and Key Words," in *Art and Meaning: Rhetoric in Biblical Literature*, ed. David J. A. Clines, David M. Gunn, and Alan J. Hauser, JSOTSup 19 (Sheffield: Sheffield Press, 1982), 37–61.

The narrative problem of Exodus, however, is also an integral part of the narrative problem of the Pentateuch, defined in the opening chapters of Genesis. Briefly stated, Genesis states the problem as God's exiling humanity from his presence, an exile caused by Adam and Eve's defilement of that presence by refusing to obey divine instruction in the garden of Eden. Subsequently, the narrative depicts God himself initiating the resolution to this problem when he instructs Abram to leave his land and to go "to the land which I will show you" (Gen. 12:1).

God's initiative with Abram includes the promise to increase his descendants, a promise intended to fill the earth with those who acknowledge the Lord (cf. Gen. 1:28), not those descendants of Adam and Eve who fill it with violence (Gen. 6:11, 13) and who desire to make a name for themselves (Gen. 11:4–5). The Lord makes such a reputation possible, but, at this time in the biblical narrative, only among the descendants of Abram: "I will make you into a great nation and I will bless you; I will make your name great, and you will be a blessing" (Gen. 12:2; cf. Gal. 3:8–9). When the promise of increase begins to take historical shape in Egypt (Ex. 1:7), Pharaoh objects to Israel's growth and forces the people into his own building projects. The brick and mortar (Ex. 1:13) used for building Pithom and Rameses recalls an earlier building project, one also dedicated to human reputation (Gen. 11:3). God had separated Abraham and his descendants from that culture; Pharaoh forces them back into that culture and its royal propaganda.

Because the narrative problem of Exodus develops the problems depicted in the opening chapters of Genesis, Pharaoh's opposition cannot be reduced to local politics. Rather Pharaoh's hostility to Israel's phenomenal growth must be read as fierce opposition to God's promised resolution of the fundamental human problem. That opposition is directed at that community uniquely created by God's special blessing, a community whose unique redemptive role among the nations, especially its unyielding growth, summons up fear and opposition (cf. Acts 12).[3] Pharaoh's actions embody the nations'[4] desire to gather against the Lord and his anointed (cf. Ps. 2:2). Exodus employs three major conflicts to develop its resolution of the narrative problem stated in the opening chapters.

### The First Conflict: Pharaoh, the Lord, and Absolute Power (Ex. 3:1–15:21)

Exodus 3:1–15:21 narrates the divine initiatives that develop the contest between Pharaoh and the Lord, mediated by Moses, the Lord's messenger to Egypt and Israel. Israel is mostly passive; extreme servitude renders them unwilling participants in Moses' mission (Ex. 5:20–21; 6:9). Their fear of Pharaoh outweighs their perception of God's mighty acts (Ex. 14:10–12). Two clusters of keywords define this struggle. The nouns and verb describing Israel's servitude[5] and the verbs describing Pharaoh's hardness of heart.

God repeatedly demands that Pharaoh let Israel go to serve him (4:23; 7:16; 8:1, 20; 9:1, 13; 10:3),[6] but Pharaoh refuses. Pharaoh hardens his heart, and God also hardens Pharaoh's

---

3. See especially Ex. 1:12, 20. Compare this episode with Acts 12 which narrates the persecution of the church after the Passover, thereby recalling the Exodus experience, and shows how persecution could not stop the growth of the Word of God (12:14; cf. 13:49–50).

4. Balak's fear of Israel's numbers and his solution (Num. 22:2–6) recalls Pharaoh's response to Israel's growth.

5. The words *'bd* and *'bdh* occur approximately 97 times in Exodus: 67 times in 1:1–15:21; 17 times in 19–24; 2 times in 32–34; and 11 times (*'bdh* only) in 35–40.

6. The keywords referring to servitude occur 33 times in the plagues pericope (7:8–11:10).

heart.[7] Pharaoh does urge Israel to serve the Lord, once before the final plague (10:24), and then after the death of the first-born (12:31), but he repents of this and pursues Israel into the sea with his army; the waters swallow them at the command of the Lord (15:7; cf. 7:12). When Israel sees the Egyptians lying dead on the shore she fears the Lord and puts her trust (4:1, 5, 8–9, 31; 14:31) in him and in his servant Moses. Pharaoh's disappearance coincides with Moses' exaltation.

The resolution of the first conflict begets Israel's praise (15:1–21). This song reminds the reader of the nations who will tremble at the passing of God's people (15:14–16); Egypt is not the only nation whose destiny is tied to what God is doing with Israel. It also introduces the establishment of the Lord's dwelling place (15:13, 17), thereby indicating that royal building activity is still within the scope of the narrative's address, but that now it shifts to the interests of the one who reigns forever (15:18). Identification of this dwelling place with "the mountain of your inheritance" anticipates the building project, which will enable the Lord's presence in Israel's midst, and the place where its design will be revealed. Because the reference to God's dwelling follows the nations' response to God's military march, the Song of the Sea picks up and anticipates a further development of the fundamental conflict between God and the nations, as stated in the opening of Genesis. Although Pharaoh's death and Israel's separation and freedom from Egypt resolves the conflict between God and Pharaoh, this does not yet resolve the problem of Exodus. Rather, it occasions the second conflict.

---

7. Pharaoh hardens his heart ten times (7:13, 14, 22; 8:11, 15, 28; 9:7, 34, 35; 13:15); the Lord also hardens Pharaoh heart ten times (4:21; 7:3, 9, 12; 10:1, 20, 27; 11:10; 14:4, 8, 17). In the context of a cosmic battle, God's hardening of Pharaoh's heart amounts to an instrument of war. We find similar language in the NT when Paul describes God as giving sinners over to their sinful desires, Rom. 1:24, 26, 28.

## The Second Conflict: Israel, God, and Complaints in the Desert (15:22–24:18)

With the conflict between God and Pharaoh resolved, the narrative develops the relationship between Israel and her new master, a relationship characterized by complaints against Moses. Israel's complaints about the lack of water at Marah and about food in the desert of Sin contrast with the plenty of Egypt (Ex. 16:3). In answer to Moses' mediation, God provides Israel with water and food with the result that, after Exodus 17:7, Israel no longer complains about her sustenance in the desert. These provisions, however, do not resolve the conflict between God and Israel because the real issue is not lack of sustenance but whether or not Israel will submit to God's law.

Israel's complaints occur in the context of the Lord's expectation that Israel submit to his law. Thus at Marah the Lord tells Israel he will not bring the diseases of Egypt upon them if they pay careful attention to his voice, commandments, and decrees (15:25–26). After Israel disobeys the Lord's instructions concerning the manna, the Lord asks Moses: "How long will you [plural] refuse to keep my commandments and instructions?" (16:28). Thus the narrative links Israel's lack of sustenance in the desert to a new theme: submission to God's instructions. In the desert pericope (Ex. 15:22–18:27) the question to be answered is not: "Who is Israel's master?" or, "Whom will Israel serve?" Rather, after Israel's liberation from Egypt the question becomes: "What is the nature of Israel's service to the LORD?" or, more existentially, "How will Israel survive outside of Egypt?" The answer is: Submit to the Lord's commands and decrees (Ex. 15:25–26; cf. Lev. 18:5; Deut. 8:3).

Legal vocabulary clustered for the most part at the beginning and ending of the pericope frames the entire desert episode.

This suggests that Israel's survival—whether she needs food or water, is oppressed by her enemies (17:8–16), or suffers internal problems (18:1–27)—depends on conformity to the instruction of the Lord.

**Table 5.1 Torah frame of the desert episode**

| Exodus | A | | A¹ |
|---|---|---|---|
| to judge (*špṭ*) | | | 18:13, 16, 22², 26² |
| judgment (*mšpṭ*) | 15:25 | | |
| to command (*ṣwh*) | | 16:16, 24, 32, 34 | 18:23 |
| commandment (*mṣwh*) | 15:26 | | |
| decree (*ḥq*) | 15:25, 26 | | 18:16, 20 |
| law (*twrh*) | 15:25 (*yrh*) | 16:4, 28 | 18:16, 20 |
| to obey (*šmʿ lql*) | 15:26 | | 18:19 (*b*), 24 |

Miraculous sustenance in the desert does not resolve the conflict between the Lord and Israel. The references to the law in the frame and the divine question in Exodus 16:28 suggest that Israel's survival in the desert does not so much depend on food and water, but on conformity to God's instructions. Without Egyptian sustenance Israel is confronted with a new form of existence: only submission to God's Word will keep her alive. There is no indication that Israel so submitted in the desert pericope; the manna episode suggests that Israel is stubborn. The resolution to the conflict about survival is narrated in Exodus 19–24. Confronted with the good things the Lord has done for her (19:4), Israel promises submission to his words (19:8), and—in consequence of the Lord's terrible descent, presence, and declaration of the law—seals her submission with a self-maledictory oath (24:3, 7). By this act of vassal submission the conflict between the Lord and Israel comes to a legal resolution. It also answers the question posed by the first conflict: "Whom will Israel serve?"

After Israel seals the covenant, Moses ascends to the top of Sinai where, in God's presence, he receives instructions for the construction of a building by which the Lord would dwell in the midst of this special people ("have them make a sanctuary for me, and I will dwell among them" [25:8]). It is while Moses receives these instructions that the third conflict occurs.

### The Third Conflict: Israel, God, and the Golden Calf (32:1–34:35)

Israel's complaints in the desert pale by comparison with her construction of the golden calf, an anti-tabernacle project[8] by which she defiles the presence of God, compromises the covenant, and exposes herself to destruction (32:10). Such divine destruction Pharaoh experienced because of his stubbornness. Israel, stubborn like Pharaoh (33:3, 5; 34:9),[9] would have been similarly consumed by God's anger had it not been for the mediator God appointed (32:11–14). Israel does not escape the consequences of her rebellion (32:27–29, 35), but God relents of his anger, forgives their sin, and renews the covenant (34:27–28). God's forgiveness brings this conflict to resolution.

8. For a brief discussion of this construction as an anti-tabernacle project, see Terence E. Fretheim, *Exodus*, Interpretation (Louisville: John Knox, 1991), 28–281. The verb 'śh occurs 323 times in Exodus, and 236 in Ex. 25–40, a key word in the instructions for the tabernacle and the description of Israel's compliance. Before Israel "makes" the tabernacle (Ex. 35:10), however, she "makes" the golden calf (32:1, 4, 8).

9. The verb which describes Israel's stubbornness (qšh) also occurs in the triad of verbs that describe Pharaoh's stubbornness (qšh, ḥzq, kbd).

This resolution, however, does not constitute the end of the narrative; divine forgiveness now makes possible what God intended for his people: participation in a royal building project (Ex. 35–39). God's grace makes possible the construction of the building central to the expression of God's kingship on earth: "Israel and the church have their existence because God picked up the pieces."[10] And because God forgave his erring and faithless people, the fire that dwells[11] in their midst does not consume them (40:34–38; cf. 3:3; 24:17). But it could have, and later did (Lev. 10:1–3; Num. 11:1–3).

The third conflict and its resolution answers the question: "Who determines Israel's construction projects?"or, "Who determines the nature of and Israel's participation in royal propaganda?" The outcome of the first conflict indicated that Pharaoh had neither the power nor the authority to force Israel to build his store cities; the conclusion of the third conflict indicates that Israel herself may not determine such projects or propaganda either. God's design will be followed (Ex. 25:9), or he will make propaganda on his own (2 Kings 17:18, 20, 23; 23:27; 24:3, 20).

10. Brevard S. Childs, *The Book of Exodus: A Critical, Theological Commentary* (Philadelphia: Westminster Press, 1974), 580. For more on the role of Ex. 32–34 in its canonical context, see also Brevard S. Childs, *Introduction to the Old Testament as Scripture* (Philadelphia: Fortress, 1979), 175–76.

11. Read in isolation from Genesis, Exodus provides no hint that the theme of the Lord's dwelling with Israel is part of its narrative agenda. Seen from the perspective of the narrative problem defined by Genesis (exile from the presence of God), and its initial resolution with the call to Abram (move toward the land, i.e., the place where the Lord would dwell), the appearance of this theme at Ex. 25:8 is not a problem. References to the land in Ex. 3:8, 17 can then be read as part of the larger trajectory that will bring Israel into the Lord's presence. That Israel finds herself in God's tabernacling presence before she gets to the land is also important: God's presence and the disclosure of Torah are pre-land realities that nevertheless are crucial for life in the land. It is in the desert, at Sinai, that God brings about a partial solution to the human problem: he ends the exile of Adam's descendants (those elected through Abraham) and teaches them to live by his Word. In this manner Israel is led to acknowledge that, like Egypt, the Promised Land has no resources to effect such a resolution (Lev. 18:1–5), claims of the local religions to the contrary.

## Summary

Closely linked together, these major conflicts move the Exodus narrative from one master and one construction project to another. The close relationship and special purpose attached to the relationship between the Lord and Israel occasioned the struggle between Pharaoh and the Lord, during which struggle Pharaoh forced Israel to construct his store cities. Freedom from Pharaoh's construction project led to Israel's complaints about sustenance in the desert. The Lord's resolution points Israel to his law. After Israel's submission at Sinai the Lord discloses his desire to dwell among his covenant people by means of a building he wants his vassals to construct according to his own design. Later, after God forgives Israel's rebellious anti-tabernacle building project, Israel constructs the various parts of the tabernacle, Moses assembles the tabernacle, and the Lord's glory cloud dwells in it.[12]

# The Structure of Exodus

Exodus is composed of a double triadic structure. In the first triad the narrative moves from Egypt into God's presence at Sinai (cf. 3:12) where the former slaves become God's vassals by means

---

12. The intimate links between the conflicts, and the move from one master and building project to another, argue against the suggestion that chapters 1–15:21 form the climax of the plot of Exodus and that as such these chapters generate meaning on the whole of the Pentateuch, as J. Severino Croatto suggests, "The Function of the Non-Fulfilled Promises: Reading the Pentateuch from the Perspective of the Latin-American Oppressed People," in *The Personal Voice in Biblical Interpretation,* ed. Ingrid Rosa Kitzberger (London: Routledge, 1999), 49–50; this thesis is worked out in greater detail in his "Exodo 1–15: Algunas claves literarias y teológicas para entender el pentateuco," *EstBib* 52 (1994): 167–94. Chapters 1–15 generate meaning within the Pentateuch as they contribute to the entire plot of Exodus. Moreover, Croatto's failure to include chapters 15:22–40:34 stifles Exodus' solution to the narrative problem stated in its opening chapters.

of a suzerain-vassal treaty. Israel does not, however, submit to this covenant until after their complaints in the desert receive God's answer. At the end of the first triad Moses ascends the mountain into God's presence where he receives the design for the instrument of God's dwelling in the midst of his people. The narrative does not move from instruction to construction, however, until God forgives Israel's apostasy and renews the covenant. After this Moses assembles the tabernacle and the glory cloud fills it.

A   Royal Conflict: From Slaves' Lament to Servants' Praise (1–15:21)
   B   The Desert: Complaints in God's presence (15:22–18:27)
A¹   The Royal Mountain: We will do all we have heard! (19:1–24:18)
C   Tabernacle and Sabbath: Let there be a sanctuary! (25:1–31:18)
   D   In God's Presence: Stubborn, Like Pharaoh (32–34)
C¹   God's Presence in the Tabernacle: And it was so! (35–40)

In this structure the sigla A–A¹ and C–C¹ point to the fundamental narrative movement in each half; B and D indicate the transitions from one aspect of this movement to the other. This structure suggests that even as B and D nuance the antecedent narratives (A and C), so they shape the audience's hearing of the subsequent narrative (A¹ and C¹). That is, the desert and the corruption narratives nuance the audience's hearing of the covenant making and the construction of the tabernacle.

### From Egypt to Sinai: From One Master to Another

Exodus 1–2 introduces the protagonists of the narrative: Israel, Pharaoh, Moses, and the Lord; they also define the narrative problem: Pharaoh's oppression of Israel and their forced participation in his building program. This oppression occasions the conflict between him and Israel's Lord. The response to this conflict begins with the call of Moses (3–4) and develops when Pharaoh rebuffs Moses and Aaron, denies knowing the Lord (5:2), refuses to let Israel go, and increases her burdens for the building program (5:1–6:1).[13] In the light of this rebuff, God confirms Moses' call and his position as God's messenger (6:2–7:7). The Pharaoh who declared that he did not know the Lord (5:2) will come to know him (7:5, 17; 8:22; 9:14) by mighty signs and plagues. Moses and Aaron let Pharaoh know the result of the plagues when Aaron's staff swallows the staffs of Pharaoh's magicians (7:8–13; "swallow": 7:12; 15:12), but Pharaoh refuses to submit. The tenth plague, embedded in the Passover narrative, forces Pharaoh to relent. He sends Israel away to serve the Lord, but he repents of this, and pursues Israel into the waters of the Sea of Reeds. The Lord manipulates the waters of judgment so that Egypt drowns and Israel passes through safely. When the people of God see their enemy dead on the seashore, they believe in the Lord and his servant Moses (14:30–31; cf. 4:1, 4, 8–9). Led by Moses and Miriam, Israel sings the Lord's praises (15:1–21).

The narrative problem enunciated in chapters 1–2 has been resolved: the Lord heard Israel's cry (2:23–25; 3:7–8) and answered with convincing signs of his power; Israel is free from servitude to Pharaoh's building program. The development and resolution of the narrative problem occur within a conceptual framework familiar to Israel: the movement of

---

13. No increase in killing of the boy babies! It is the building program that is crucial for Pharaoh.

lament to praise.[14] The psalm of praise, then, effectively concludes the narrative.[15]

> Lament—Oppression and enforced construction: 1–2
>> Moses' call: 3:1–7:7
>> Signs and plagues: 7:8–11:10
>> Tenth plague and the Passover: 12:1–13:16
>> Passage through the Sea: 13:17–14:31
> Praise—Song of the Sea: 15:1–21

Although Pharaoh's death provides a fitting conclusion and
opportunity for Israel's praise, the journey begun on Passover
night (12:37) moves beyond the sea and into the wilderness
(15:22), where Israel wanders for some months (16:1; 17:1; cf.
19:2). The narrative move into the desert is a further development of the promise that God would take Israel to the Promised
Land (3:7–11), away from Egypt. But it will be some time before
Israel enters into that Promised Land. Her stay in the desert
depicts a time of complaint and instruction which introduces
the theme of learning to depend upon her Redeemer and to
break dependence on Egypt (cf. 16:3). By moving Israel into
the inhospitable desert God has led her into a new living space
where she can survive only by divine provision of water, manna,
and protection from the nations represented by Amalek. In two
sections the Exodus desert epoch memorializes Israel's murmur-
ing against God and his servant Moses (15:22–17:7), and the

14. On the lament pattern as a basis for understanding Exodus 1–15:21 as a
unit, see James Plastaras, *The God of Exodus: The Theology of the Exodus Narratives*
(Milwaukee: Bruce Publishing Co., 1966), 49–57, and C. Westermann, *Praise and
Lament in the Psalms*, trans. Keith R. Crim and Richard N. Soulen (Atlanta: John
Knox, 1981), 260.

15. Other psalms that close a narrative: Gen. 49; 2 Sam. 22; 23:1–7. Psalms that
are part of a narrative opening: 1 Sam. 2:1–10; Luke 1:46–55; 67–79.

embarrassing praise of God and wise administration offered by the Gentile Jethro, Moses' father-in-law (17:8–18:27). The wilderness experiences before Sinai depict a transition from one state of being to another. Pharaoh is gone; now Israel begins to learn what it means to be the servant of the Redeemer.

This transition betrays the liminal characteristics of a rite of passage: Israel is separated from its Egyptian past, and is waiting to be taken up into a future reality, the covenant at Sinai. This transitional space and time is one of "betwixt and between," a space and time when the old order is gone and the new is not yet; it is without norm yet forms part of a tightly structured universe; it can give way to antinomianism directed against the laws and values that hold society together.[16] The liminal zone "is frequently likened to death, to being in the womb, to invisibility, to darkness, to bisexuality, to the wilderness, and to an eclipse of the sun or moon."[17] Those in the transition are on the threshold of new life, but have not yet arrived. For these "threshold people," it is a time of "emptiness at the center."[18]

Israel's complaints in the Exodus wilderness epoch are typical liminal behavior, Moses is typical of the ritual experts that accompany the "threshold people," and Israel's new life is anticipated by the legal frame around the desert narrative and the divine question: "How long will you [pl.] refuse to keep my commandments and instructions?" (16:28).

The journey begun on Passover night (12:37) ends at Sinai three months later (19:2).[19] This last of the itinerary notices

---

16. Victor W. Turner, *Dramas, Fields and Metaphors: Symbolic Action in Human Society* (Ithaca, NY: Cornell University Press, 1974), 13–14.

17. Victor W. Turner, *The Ritual Process: Structure and Anti-Structure* (Chicago: Aldine, 1969), 95.

18. Ibid., 127 (quoting Martin Buber).

19. See Arie C. Leder, "The Desert Itinerary Notices of Exodus: Their Narrative, Semiotic, and Theological Functions," *EstBib* (forthcoming).

in Exodus links Sinai with the Passover night in Egypt (Ex. 12:37a; 13:20; 14:1ff.; 15:22; 16:1; 17:1; 19:2). Israel remains in the wilderness, but with 19:1–2 the narrative begins to focus on a specific location: *the* mountain (19:2; cf. 3:12). The use of the definite article recalls the mountain where God revealed himself to Moses, the mountain of which he said "you" (pl.) will serve me there (3:12). "Mountain" becomes the narrative icon which lends meaning to the covenanting at Sinai. With 19:3 begins the account of Moses' ascents into and descents from the presence of God during which he receives and transmits to Israel the Lord's words. Israel is not allowed to touch the mountain nor ascend into God's immediate presence, on pain of death (19:12–13; cf. 20:18–19). In God's dangerous presence Israel receives God's offer of covenant and vows covenant obedience (19:8; 24:3, 7) with a self-maledictory oath (24:8). Israel has formally submitted itself to another master. No longer is there any doubt about whom Israel will serve, or who is Israel's master. After this, Moses alone ascends into the glory cloud and stays there for forty days and forty nights (24:18).

Moses' ascents and descents[20] in chapters 19 and 24 frame the covenant instruction material (20:1–17; 21:1–23:19) and embed it in a narrative which depicts the presence of a God Israel has heretofore not experienced. His fiery presence motivates Israel's obedience and warns against faithlessness (20:18–20). Moses' final ascent brings him into the presence of God which "looked like a consuming fire" (24:17).

---

20. Moses' ascents to and descents from Sinai continue up to and including Exodus 34. For example, Rolf P. Knierim, "The Composition of the Pentateuch," in *Seminar Papers: The Society of Biblical Literature Annual Meeting* (Atlanta: Scholars Press, 1985), 400–403, argues that this pattern organizes Exodus 19:3–39:43. However, the speeches in 25–31 are instructions for the building of God's dwelling, not covenant stipulations or instruction.

---

### MOUNTAIN

Mountains are an important element in ancient Near Eastern religion. The Egyptians speak of the "glorious hill of the primordial beginning"; the top of the *ziggurat* at Larsa is called "house of the bond between heaven and earth" (Keel, *The Symbolism of the Biblical World*, 113).

God appears to Israel at the top of Mount Sinai not because it is holy per se, but because he has chosen it as the place of his revelation. The tabernacle, and later the temple on Mount Zion, takes over this function. Although barely a hill, Isaiah describes Mt. Zion as "chief among the mountains; it will be raised among the hills" (Isa. 2:2). The place of God's dwelling discloses the crucial bond between heaven and earth, the temple in the Old Testament, the church in the New (1 Cor. 3:16).

---

The mountain of self-disclosure and Israel's vow: 19:1–25
    Instruction: 20:1–17
    Fear of God's presence: 20:18–26
    Instruction: 21:1–23:33
The mountain of self-disclosure and Israel's vow: 24:1–18

Israel is now formally God's people; they have acknowledged him as their overlord and vowed to live by his instructions, not Pharaoh's. The first triad suggests that Egypt and Sinai form the two poles of Israel's identity, that she must continue her journey away from vassaldom to Egypt and affirm her loyalty to the God of Sinai. In effect, Israel is invited to see herself as a threshold people: away from Egypt in the wilderness, but not yet arrived at Sinai.

The element of construction, definitive of Israel's identity in Egypt, is developed in the next triad. Israel will now serve (*'bd*) the Lord's royal propaganda interests as she served (*'bd*) Pharaoh's by building a monument to God's victory over Egypt.

### From Instruction to Compliance: Construction of the Sanctuary

The Lord's first speech to Moses on Sinai picks up and develops the theme of royal construction: the building of a sanctuary for the Lord's dwelling in Israel's midst (25:8–9). Recalling the creation account,[21] there follow six speeches detailing the offerings, the specifications for the sanctuary furnishings and the sanctuary, the design of the priestly appurtenances and the instructions for their consecration, and instructions for the builders Bezalel and Oholiab (25:1–31:11). The seventh speech (31:12–17) reminds Israel to observe the Sabbath as a sign for the generations to come "so that you may know that I am the LORD, who makes you holy" (31:13). Thus every Sabbath reminds Israel of her priestly identity ("kingdom of priests and a holy nation," Ex. 19:5), an identity essential to her temple building responsibilities. Because the building instructions are organized in the 6 + 1 format of the creation account, they recall what should have been: humanity serving God in his holy presence (Gen. 2:1–3). They also anticipate what will be: renewed humanity in the presence of God (Rev. 21:22–27; 22:14)—but not yet.

When God brought Israel to himself (19:4), he kept her at a safe distance, lest the people die (19:12–13). Now he will dwell in *Israel's midst*. The seven speeches make it clear that the Lord's dwelling place in the people's midst will maintain the distances defined at Sinai: a court, Israel at the foot of the mountain; a holy place for the priests, halfway up the mountain; and a most

---

21. See Peter J. Kearney, "Creation and Liturgy: The P Redaction of Ex 25–40," *ZAW* 89 (1977): 375–87.

holy place for the high priests, Moses at the top of Sinai. Israel's sinful nature requires the distance; God's grace designs an "incarnational" medium by which the distance is minimized and the nearness maximized so that he might meet with his people. With the tabernacle God is creating space for his people to know and enjoy him forever (29:43–46; John 1:14).

Throughout 25–31 Moses remains in God's presence at the top of Sinai. Then the narrative abruptly shifts to the people who are awaiting Moses at the foot of Sinai (32:1). There, motivated by the people's impatient waiting for Moses, Aaron has presided over the construction of a calf in whose presence Israel worships God with a mixture of prescribed and alien elements (32:6). Israel's corrupt worship in the Lord's presence brings on his wrath. Only Moses' intercession in God's immediate presence saves all Israel from God's anger (32:7–14; cf. 3:2–5). As he descends, Moses breaks the tablets of the law, indicating Israel's violation of the covenant, and 3000 Israelites die at the hands of the Levites (32:15–29).

When Moses pleads for pardon (32:30ff.), he is told that the sinners will die for their rebellion (32:33), and that God will not accompany Israel to the Promised Land, for their stubbornness ("stiff-necked," 33:3, 5; 34:9; cf. 32:9) may provoke divine destruction.[22] Moses pleads for God's continuing presence among his people and that he show him his glory. The Lord grants Moses' requests and speaks mercifully to him (33:12–23). Moses then prepares two new stone tablets upon which he writes the words of the covenant (34:1–4, 27–28). The Lord reveals his compassionate and gracious nature to Moses: he is slow to anger, but will not let the guilty go unpunished (34:6–7). This

---

22. The narrative describes Israel with vocabulary reminiscent of Pharaoh's hardness of heart: see the verb *qšh* in Ex. 7:3 and 13:15 and the adjective in 1:14 and 6:9. How does Israel hear this?

compassionate and gracious God then renews the covenant and forgives his stubborn people. Moses again descends, this time with the tablets of the renewed covenant. Thereafter, whenever Moses consults with God in his presence, he veils his face to protect Israel from the full glory of God (34:29–35).

The narrative time between God's instruction and Israel's construction of the tabernacle reveals Israel's true nature: stiff-necked and apostate, a people in deep need of God's compassion and grace. It depicts God's second deliverance of Israel, this time from herself. Now she is free from Pharaoh and forgiven by God. It is this forgiven people that builds God's dwelling place.

After the golden calf episode Moses assembles the community and repeats the instructions for the offerings necessary for building the tabernacle (35:4–19; cf. 25:1–7). Israel willingly offers more than necessary and, under the leadership of Bezalel and Oholiab, begins the building project (35:20–36:7). Israel obediently manufactures all the necessary items for the tabernacle, ending with the gold plate for Aaron's turban, upon which is inscribed: "Holy to the LORD" (36:8–39:31). Then, in a narrative evocative of Genesis 1:31–2:3, Israel completes the work of the tabernacle in perfect obedience, and brings all the items to Moses (39:32–41), who blesses them (39:42–43). They are now a consecrated (31:13) and blessed (39:43) people, true signs of the Sabbath (Gen. 2:3). No longer slaves who build Pharaoh's store cities, they are priestly servants who participated in the building of the Lord's throne room.

Moses assembles and consecrates the tabernacle and the priesthood on the first day of the first month in the second year (40:2, 17; cf. 12:1; Gen. 6:13). After Moses completes his work (40:33), the glory of the Lord fills the sanctuary: God is in the midst of his forgiven people and he will lead them on their journey (40:34–38).

112

Like the first, the second triad places Israel's true identity between two poles, this time between instruction and compliance. It invites Israel to continue her journey, this time from instruction to compliance and so to affirm her loyalty to the God who renewed his covenant with her. In effect, Israel is invited to see herself, again, as a threshold people, instructed at the mountain, but not yet fully compliant. The journey would never be complete, not even in the land (2 Kings 17:18, 20, 23; 23:27; 24:3, 20).

## Waiting for the Land

At the end of Exodus the royal slaves have become royal servants; their Lord and Master in their midst. But they are still at Sinai; they won't leave for another year. That leaving and the further journeys are anticipated at the end of Exodus: "whenever the cloud lifted from above the tabernacle, they would set out . . . during all their travels" (40:36–38). Thus, at the end of Exodus, Israel is still waiting for the land. But she is waiting for that promised future in the presence of the Lord.

Echoing the garden of Eden account, the end of Exodus suggests that Israel has arrived at, and received, a gift greater than the land, the presence of God. That Sinai presence, "incarnate" in the wilderness tabernacle, creates new space where God's people may freely serve him according to his instructions, and where they are free from the enforced building of cities whose foundations are of this world. In the wilderness, as far from Egypt as she is from Canaan, God has brought her home, to himself. At this wilderness mountain, far from the pressures of the nations, God will teach her again how to live in his presence. The space God creates must first receive a certain shape, for life in God's presence on the way to the land will be one of sacrifice, cleanliness, and holiness. Israel's waiting at Sinai is a time of instruction, of preparation for contact with the nations in the Promised Land. At Sinai God's people are safe.

For the time being the promise of land is partially fulfilled by the building emblematic of God's kingdom rule: the royal throne room in a tent. This presence reminds Israel that her identity is rooted in Sinai's instruction, not Egypt's or Canaan's ways of life; that her vocation consists in being priestly participants in a royal propaganda that is not of this world. This is not the waiting of exasperation, but of pedagogy, of discipleship, of sanctification.

The journey to the promised future continues for God's people today. As in the days of Exodus, the land itself is not crucial, God's presence is. Thus the church awaits a greater fulfillment of the promise of land (Heb. 4), led by the one who is God's presence in its midst, Jesus Christ (Matt. 1:23; 28:20b; John 1:14). During this journey she must not leave God's presence, for the space God has created through Christ and the Holy Spirit continues to be shaped by sacrifice, cleanliness, and holiness (Rom. 12:1–2; 2 Cor. 6:14–7:1). Only thus, and in God's time, will those freed from the enforced building of the cities of this world enter the space redemptively created for them (Rev. 21:27; 22:14–15).

# 6

# Leviticus: Priestly Instruction for Life in God's Presence

**Summary.** From the Tent of Meeting and through Moses, God instructs Israel in the sacrifices of atonement. The Lord instructs and Moses ordains Aaron. When Aaron presents the offering, fire from the Lord consumes it and Israel responds in joy. Aaron's sons Nadab and Abihu are consumed by fire when they offer an unauthorized sacrifice. Through Moses the Lord instructs Israel to distinguish between clean and unclean animals for their food, and gives them instructions for cleanliness and the Day of Atonement. Israel must be holy to the Lord and distinguish herself from the practices of the nations. Her priests receive specific regulations for their holiness. Moses instructs Israel in Sabbath care of the land. Israel's obedience will bring about the Lord's presence in the people's midst; disobedience brings about expulsion from the land. These are the instructions the Lord gives Moses on Mt. Sinai.

**Central narrative interest.** Through Moses God instructs Israel for living safely in his presence as a sacrificial, clean, and holy people (Lev. 18:1–5).

115

## Leviticus as a Narrative

While commentary literature on Leviticus acknowledges the presence of narrative in Leviticus (8–10; 24:10–23), it seldom goes beyond that in consideration of the book's narrative character. Indeed, at first glance Leviticus appears to be no more than a collection of priestly instructions without a story to tell. Gordon J. Wenham points out, however, that the repeated introductory clause, "And the LORD spoke to Moses," places these speeches within the narrative framework[1] that is part of the Sinai event (7:37–38; 26:46; 27:34). But, how can so much speech and so little narrative function as part of the larger narrative?

The question of the relationship between narrative and law arose in the course of source-critical analysis of the Pentateuch; the explosion of legal material at Exodus 19 collided with then current understandings of historical narration. Extraction of sources allowed for the "normal" histories of J(ahwist) and E(lohist), but P(riestly) material remained problematic. How could lists, dates, and legal, building, and cultic instructions tell a story? When P was accepted as the late product of legalistic post-exilic thought, and thus not true to Israel's religious genius, the problem could be safely ignored.

Several solutions to the problem of mixed genres have been suggested. James W. Watts, for example, argues that lists form the primary organizational principle for the priestly material in the Pentateuch. Thus, lists "specify the implications of the story," and the interposed narratives, such as are found in Exodus 32–34, function as warnings to the community.[2] Commentators

---

1. Gordon J. Wenham, *The Book of Leviticus*, NICOT (Grand Rapids: Eerdmans, 1979), 5–6.

2. James W. Watts, *Reading Law: The Rhetorical Shaping of the Pentateuch* (Sheffield: Sheffield Academic, 1999), 51, 53–54. See Terence E. Fretheim, *Exodus*, Interpreta-

on Job have similarly tried to relate the speeches of Job and his miserable friends to the so-called originally independent narrative framework. Is there an underlying unity in spite of the differences between the poetry and story? Rather than accept a genetic solution, Norman C. Habel,[3] focuses on the nature of narrative using Robert Alter's discussion of the relationship between narration and dialogue[4] to propose a narrative reading of Job.

Biblical narrative, Alter argues, is composed of two elements: a third-person description of the past account and speech. In terms of proportions "third-person narration is frequently only a bridge between much larger units of direct speech." Because of this commitment to speech within biblical narrative, Alter suggests a "bias of stylization in the Bible's narration-through-dialogue." Acknowledging that Job's opening episodes demonstrate this combination, Habel goes on to point to narrative commentary scattered throughout (Job 1:22; 2:10; 31:40c), and to suggest that Job has a narrative plot composed of three parts: 1:1–2:10; 2:11–31:40; 32:1–42:17).

These discussions are suggestive for thinking about Leviticus as part of the larger pentateuchal narrative. Thus we note that all of Leviticus' speeches begin with narrative introductions, nine speeches conclude with narrative commentary, and the narrative sections (8–10; 24:10–23) are typical of the narrative-speech combination. We will comment briefly on each.

---

tion (Louisville: John Knox, 1991), 201–7, for a discussion of the combination of narrative and law in Exodus.

3. Norman C. Habel, *The Book of Job*, OTL (Philadelphia: Westminster, 1985), 25–27.

4. Robert Alter, *The Art of Biblical Narrative* (New York: Basic, 1985), 63–87, esp. 65 and 69.

The narrative introductions of Leviticus,[5] including those of the larger narrative sections, employ a verbal construction whose unique function is to create a verbal sequence that tells the story. Thus after Leviticus 1:1 begins with "The LORD called Moses, and he spoke to him from the Tent of Meeting," we have a series of speeches, each of which begins with "the LORD spoke to Moses." Together these speeches, with their narrative introductions, form the story of God's instructions to Israel about how to live sacrificially in his presence, keeping themselves undefiled and holy. In doing so, however, Leviticus also continues the narrative of divine instruction begun in Exodus, at other places of divine self-disclosure: the burning bush, the mountain, the cloud on the mountain, and finally the cloud and the Tent (Ex. 40:34–35). Leviticus then consists in another series of divine instructions, introduced like that in Exodus 19:3 ("and the LORD called to [Moses] from the mountain and said") and Exodus 3:4 ("God called to [Moses] from within the bush . . . and said"). As in Exodus, so the speeches in Leviticus specify, as Watts argues, the implications of the basic narrative: the story of God bringing Israel into his presence. The only real difference is the length of the speech units: they are short in Exodus 3, get longer in Exodus 19–24, and longer still in Exodus 25–31, 35–39, and Leviticus.

The instructions in Leviticus also conclude with narrative commentary (7:35–38; 10:20; 13:59; 14:54–57; 15:32–33; 16:34c; 21:24; 23:44; 24:23; 26:46; 27:34), including the larger narrative sections. These conclusions serve to indicate the place where Israel received these instructions, Sinai; to summa-

5. 1:1; 4:1; 5:14; 6:1, 8, 19, 24; 7:22, 28; 8:1; 11:1; 12:1; 13:1; 14:1; 15:1; 16:1–2a; 17:1; 18:1; 19:1; 20:1; 21:1, 16; 22:1, 17, 26; 23:1, 9, 23, 26, 33; 24:1, 10; 25:1; 26:1.

rize the instructions and to emphasize that they are the Lord's commands; to recall the authoritative role of Moses and his obedience or others' to him; and to warn of the consequences of taking God's holiness for granted. These functions fit Alter's observation that "narration is . . . often relegated to the role of confirming assertions made in dialogue—occasionally . . . with an explanatory gloss."[6] Watts's suggestion that interposed narratives in priestly material serve as warning places the longer narrative sections in the same category. Does the extended narration-dialogue narrative develop a plot? We will begin to answer that question with a discussion of the link between Leviticus and Exodus.

## Connection with Antecedent Narrative

Taking Leviticus as a narration-dialogue complex whose speeches are embedded in a story line typical of Hebrew narrative, we now move to its connection with the antecedent Exodus narrative. Leviticus opens with the clause, "The LORD called Moses," that stands in syntactical continuity with its antecedent in Exodus 40:34, "Then the cloud covered the Tent of Meeting and the glory of the LORD filled the tabernacle." Moving from Exodus to Leviticus we would read: "Then the cloud covered the Tent of Meeting and the glory of the LORD filled the tabernacle, but Moses could not enter the Tent of Meeting because the cloud had settled upon it, . . . The LORD called Moses and spoke to him from the Tent of Meeting" (Ex. 40:34–35; Lev. 1:1).

6. Alter, *The Art of Biblical Narrative*, 65. The function of Lev. 8–10 and 24:10–23 will be discussed in greater detail below. For narrative introductions, conclusions, and interludes in Exodus, especially their functions, see Watts, *Reading Law*, 50.

The material in Exodus 40:36–38 is disjunctive to the narrative being told; it does not recount the past, but refers to a repeated action in the future, to what Israel would do once it left Sinai (similarly, Num. 10:11, in the usual form for narration of the past). This interruption of past narration provides a formal closure to the Exodus narrative. Nevertheless, the typical Hebrew sequence for past narration in Exodus 40:34 and Leviticus 1:1 provide narrative continuity for the Sinai event: divine self-disclosure for purposes of instruction.

Because Moses receives this divine instruction from the building whose construction and indwelling constitutes the resolution of Exodus' narrative problem, Leviticus also addresses fundamental elements of the narrative problem of the Pentateuch: exile from God's presence and the human need for divine instruction. Although God is now present among his people by means of the Tent, he does not speak directly to Israel, but communicates only through Moses. The distance between God and his people, required by his holiness and Israel's unclean state (cf. Ex. 19:12–13; 20:18–21; 24:2), constitutes the narrative problem which Leviticus addresses; the location of the divine dwelling and the speeches of instruction given to Moses together bridge the distance and enable the people to dwell safely in God's consuming-fire presence.

The clue to this definition of the narrative problem is found in the form of the opening clauses of Leviticus 1:1 and the similar clauses earlier in Exodus 24:16; 19:3; 3:4.[7] Comparison of these clauses discloses that Leviticus shares in the resolution to the narrative problem of the Pentateuch.

7. Rolf Rendtorff (*Leviticus*, Biblischer Kommentar III.1 [Neukirchener Verlag, 1985], 16–17) argues that Lev. 1:1 is a redactional device which introduces the second large complex of instructions after Exodus 25:1, and that the form of this clause is also found elsewhere in Exodus (19:3; 24:16).

## The Fundamental Problem of
## the Pentateuch and Leviticus:
## Uncleanness in the Presence of God

In the opening words, "The LORD called Moses and spoke to him from the Tent of Meeting," the important aspects are the subject, "the LORD"; what he does, the verb "to call"; and the location from which he speaks, "from the Tent of Meeting." This sequence of divine self-disclosure occurs elsewhere in Exodus. Thus: "On the seventh day *the LORD called* Moses *from within the cloud*" (Ex. 24:16); the cloud was the locus of God's self-disclosure before the Tent of Meeting took over its function. Earlier still: "and *the LORD called* to him *from the mountain*" (Ex. 19:3); the mountain was the locus of divine self-disclosure before the cloud covered its top (Ex. 24:15). Finally, Moses' first meeting with the Lord at the mountain of God is described thus: "When the LORD saw he [Moses] had gone over to look, *God called* to him *from within the bush*" (Ex. 3:4); the bush was the first locus of divine self-disclosure in Exodus.

The repetition of these elements throughout Exodus and into Leviticus discloses the crucial role of Sinai in the Leviticus narrative-dialogue complex. Thus, even though the Tent is now the place of divine self-disclosure, Leviticus 7:38; 25:1; 26:46; 27:34 remind Israel that these instructions are rooted in Mt. Sinai,[8] not only as the place where God gave Moses these instructions, but also because neither Egypt nor Canaan

---

8. The mountain is a crucial metaphor which Israel shares with the ANE. The top of the mountain is understood to be the meeting place between heaven and earth, the place from which the gods make known their cosmic will. Sinai is such for Israel. The top is the place where God is enthroned (Ex. 24:10) and from which he declares his sovereign and cosmic will. The Tent of Meeting receives such importance by transference; it is, as it were, a portable mountain. See Othmar Keel, *The Symbolism*

may be the source of instruction for Israel's life in God's presence (Lev. 18:1–5). Forever in Israel's past, Sinai is the only source of divine instruction. The Tent is a temporary instrument, a "mobile mountain" that facilitates God's presence among his people on the way to the land. Once in the land God will have Solomon construct his dwelling place on another mountain: Zion, from where the law will go forth to all nations (Isa. 2:3).

Although God himself brought Israel into his presence (Ex. 19:4), there remains a distance between them and the place God chooses to reveal himself. Moreover, God does not speak directly to them, only through Moses. Any compromise of this distance brings death (Ex. 19:12, 13–21; cf. Num. 1:53; 12:6–8). This distance from God is a consequence of the fundamental conflict between God and humanity, a conflict originating in the Garden of Eden. In the garden God spoke to Adam and Eve without the mediation of priests, and he instructed them not to eat the fruit from a particular tree. Eve acknowledged this instruction when she told the serpent that God had said, "You must not touch it, or you will die" (Gen. 3:3). Nevertheless, she and Adam disobeyed, touched the fruit, and so defiled themselves. Since the unclean cannot remain in the presence of God and live, they were expelled from the garden and died in their sin (cf. Eph. 2:1).

After Adam and Eve hide among the trees we read: "But *the* LORD *God called* to the man: 'Where are you?' " (Gen. 3:9). From the point of view of the sequence of self-disclosure in Leviticus 1:1 and its antecedents in Exodus, we expect this question to be about instruction. The subsequent question— "Who told you that you were naked?"—lets the reader know

---

*of the Biblical World: Ancient Near Eastern Iconography and the Book of Psalms*, trans. Timothy J. Hallett (New York: Seabury, 1978), 113–20.

this is correct, but that in this case it is about alien instruction, for Adam and Eve only know about their nakedness as a result of surrendering to the serpent's interpretation of divine instruction. From the point of view of Leviticus 1:1 the clause "the LORD called to the man" also suggests that the matter of divine self-disclosure for purposes of instruction did not begin in Exodus 3, but in the Garden and that, therefore, the instructions of Leviticus address the conflict of instructions rooted in the event of our ancestors' failure to heed God's word.[9]

**Table 6.1 Divine self-disclosures in reverse order**

| | |
|---|---|
| The *LORD called* to Moses and spoke to him *from the Tent of Meeting* | Lev. 1:1 |
| The *LORD called* Moses *from within the cloud* | Ex. 24:16 |
| The *LORD called* to him *from the mountain* | Ex. 19:3 |
| *God called* to him *from within the bush* | Ex. 3:4 |
| The *LORD GOD called* to the man | Gen. 3:9 |

Because they are expelled from the garden for their uncleanness, Adam and his descendants no longer have access to a place of divine self-disclosure. All now live in a constant state of ignorance of God's instructions (Gen. 2:4–11:26). This ignorance leads to God's beginning a new history of instruction with Abraham, which by the end of Exodus produces a unique place of self-disclosure at Sinai that evokes the Garden. There Israel hears the voice of her Lord, although now through the mediation of

9. The prepositional phrase like "from the garden" is of course absent. But Adam and Eve are still in the garden, the place of divine self-disclosure. The need for a place of divine self-disclosure arises precisely because humanity is expelled from God's presence.

Moses and the priesthood. God's speech from these places of self-disclosure in Exodus, and ultimately the Tent of Meeting, partially solves the problem of humanity's expulsion from the presence of God, at least for a select community, Abraham's descendants. At the beginning of Leviticus it is these descendants of Abraham who are in God's presence, hearing the voice of the Lord, as it were, at the entrance to the garden of Eden.

Defilement as the result of touching the forbidden, and thus failing to heed the Lord's instruction as in Genesis 3, is a fundamental theme of Leviticus (Lev. 5:2–3; 6:18, 27; 7:19, 21; 11:8; 12:4; 15:5, 7, 10, 11, 12, 19, 21, 22, 27; 22:5, 6). Leviticus 15:31 also links such defilement to the Tent of Meeting when it says: "You must keep the Israelites separate from the things that make them unclean, so they will not die in their uncleanness *for defiling my dwelling place*, which is among them" (cf. Lev. 20:3; Num. 5:3). Defilement of God's dwelling places brings about death for humanity. Thus God's dwelling in the midst of Israel creates a problem: How can an unclean people survive in God's presence? That is the problem the divine instructions of Leviticus partially resolves.

In sum, humanity's uncleanness in God's presence, defined at the beginning of the Pentateuch, constitutes the narrative problem which also drives Leviticus' concerns. From the locus of self-revelation described in Leviticus 1:1 back to Exodus 24:16; 19:3; 3:4 and to Genesis 3:9, there is a consistent sequence that links Leviticus to this fundamental conflict. Leviticus provides a partial solution to this uncleanness by means of divine instruction from the Tent of Meeting, which, if Israel obeys, will enable her to dwell safely in the presence of God, unlike the other descendants of Adam and Eve who remain outside of God's redemptive presence.

## Leviticus and the Plot of the Pentateuch

The opening chapters of the Pentateuch not only define the conflict addressed by Leviticus, they also throw light on the mode of that resolution: Adam and Eve failed to heed divine instruction in the Garden; now at the foot of Sinai God instructs their descendants through Abraham in proper cult and conduct. Though brief, submission to the divine instruction in the Garden was a matter of life and death; in Leviticus this is massively the case. Narrative retreats, the divine voice takes over: forgiveness and purification require sacrifice; separation from the nations requires a unique diet and severe cleanliness in body and soul; and because God is holy, Israel must be holy in cult and in conduct. Thus Leviticus addresses the fundamental conflict of humanity's exile from God's presence and provides a partial solution: in God's redemptive presence a new humanity receives instructions for a new beginning.

At this point in the pentateuchal plot development, instruction assumes a large proportion for the simple reason that prescription, not description, is required: in that intimate desert presence Israel hears God's own voice, as Adam in Eden, only this time through a select messenger and because of what happened in Eden. Hearing so much instruction from God's own mouth creates a "rhetorical force" which "motivates allegiance and obedience to the law,"[10] initially necessary because of Eden, but more recently because of the golden calf incident. Narrative appears now and then to link the speeches to Sinai, or as "free-floating narratives" in support of the instruction,[11] including those of Exodus.

The covenant instructions of Exodus 19–24 and the instruction-compliance material in Exodus 25–31 and 35–40 moved the pentateuchal plot to God's tabernacling presence in Israel's

10. Watts, *Reading Law*, 71.
11. Ibid., 87. More on Lev. 8–10 and 24:10–23 below.

midst. As such they are crucial to understanding Leviticus' participation in the plot development of the Pentateuch. But there are important differences between the instructions of Exodus and Leviticus. The instructions of Exodus 19–24 are covenant stipulations which focus on the loyalty of the vassal to the suzerain. By swearing a self-maledictory oath (Ex. 24:3, 8; cf. 19:8), Israel submits herself unconditionally to be the Lord's people. She is no longer Pharaoh's vassal people, as Israel's foremen described themselves (*'bdym*, 5:15–16). Having defeated Pharaoh, the Lord now makes Pharaoh's former slaves his own with a formal covenant oath.[12] The instructions of Exodus 25–31 distinguish themselves from the covenant stipulations as building instructions. Through them God designs redemptively consecrated space to dwell with his people and lead them from Egypt and Sinai (Ex. 29:44–46; 40:36–38) to the land of promise.

God's descent into Israel's midst moves the narrative from a vertical to a horizontal plane. That is, the Tent's presence redefines Israel's living space, the camp (Lev. 15:31; 20:3; [4:12, 21; 6:11; 8:17; 9:11; 10:4–5; 13:46; 14:3, 8; 16: 26–28; 24:10, 14, 23]; cf. Num. 5:3 and, subsequently with respect to the land, Num. 35:34). The divinely indwelt camp is a microcosm of the new creation before sin: the redeemed of the Lord live there, but can only do so by heeding all the divine instructions for life in that space, lest they die in their disobedience and uncleanness (cf. Lev. 8:35; 10:2; 15:31b; 20:1–16; Gen. 2:15–17). Out-

---

12. The narrator does not describe Israel as Pharaoh's vassals. Rather, he recognizes they are the Lord's servants by Abrahamic covenant (Ex. 2:23–25). If the Sinai covenant is a renewal of the Abrahamic covenant, it renews the covenant made in Gen. 17, not 15, in the light of the threat posed by Pharaoh. However, similar threats by Abimelech to Isaac (Gen. 26) and Balak to Israel (Num. 22–24) do not lead to a covenant renewal. The Sinai covenant is unique in that it formalizes the relationship between the Lord and a people, a socio-political unit unlike the clan (*byt-'b*). Anticipating this, Exodus describes the problem between Israel and Egypt as a conflict of peoples (*'m*, 1:9, 22).

side this space is the desert, the place of uncleanness and death (Lev. 13:46; 24:10–23; Rev. 21:27; 22:15). In contrast to the covenant instructions that define Israel's loyalty, the instructions of Leviticus organize the divinely indwelt camp such that God's people may safely dwell in God's gracious but dangerous presence. Thus sacrificial, cleanliness, and holiness regulations shape life in the camp as did God's instructions to Adam in the garden. Similarly, failure to heed these instructions will result in disorder in the camp (Lev. 12–15; 19), in death (Lev. 10:1–3; 24:10–13), and ultimately expulsion from the divine presence (Lev. 18:24–28; 20:22–24; 26:14–45, esp. 41a).

## Divine Torah: By Instruction You Will Live in My Presence

Not seldom do readers of the Pentateuch confuse the emphasis on instruction with the Old Testament form of salvation. There are two problems with this. First, the instructions of Exodus and Leviticus are not impersonal codes; they are divine speech, the textually embedded voice of God. Second, these instructions appear after God rescues his people from Egypt and brings them to Sinai and, therefore, do not have as their goal the salvation of Israel. Rather, God speaks to them about the new mode of their existence in his presence, about the life of sanctification. Obedience to divine torah—the Hebrew noun for instruction—yields life in God's presence; failure to do so leads to death.

Adam and Eve's refusal of torah led to their expulsion from God's presence and death. Shortly after leaving Egypt Israel begins to learn that only the divine torah will keep her alive in the desert (Ex. 15:25–26; 16:28). Leviticus makes the point when the Lord instructs Moses to tell the Israelites:

> You must not do as they do in Egypt, where you used to live, and you must not do as they do in the land of Canaan, where I am bringing you. Do not follow their practices. You must obey my laws and be careful to follow my decrees. I am the LORD your God. Keep my decrees and laws, for the man who obeys them will live by them. I am the LORD. (Lev. 18:3–5; cf. Deut. 8:3)

Neither Egypt with all its wisdom nor Canaan with its gods on the great mountain of the north may be the source of instruction for Israel's life. Only Sinai, deep in the desert and far from all the nations of the earth, is the source of Israel's instruction, and that only because the Lord selected it as the place to teach his people. Neither the place of slavery nor the place of "sojourning" may be the source of Israel's life, for both are characterized by disorder and uncleanness, as are all the nations. Israel herself has no such resources either. Only the Lord who brought them to himself (Ex. 19:4) gives life through the instruction he speaks at Sinai and subsequently at the Tent of Meeting.

For Israel on the way to the promised future, Leviticus represents the continuing torah from Sinai-Tent of Meeting. Throughout this journey this divine voice instructs the people how to live in the Lord's presence without fear of death. Centuries later Jesus would depreciate Sinai, now the temple on Mt. Zion, when he said to the woman at the well: "Believe me, woman, the time is coming when you will worship the Father neither on this mountain nor in Jerusalem" (John 4:21). By that time the voice from Sinai had become embedded not only textually in the Torah, but had become incarnate in Christ himself (John 1:1). Thus the church continues to hear: "This is my Son, whom I love; with him I am well pleased. Listen to him!" (Matt. 17:5).

# Uncleanness in the Presence of God Illustrated: Leviticus 8–10 and 24:10–23

Two narrative sections, Leviticus 8–10 and 24:10–23, illustrate the problem of human uncleanness in the presence of God, the means by which the conflict is addressed, and death as the consequence for failure to obey the divine instructions. Leviticus 8–10 narrates the preparation for and ordination to the priesthood of Aaron and his sons, the successful beginning of the cult, and the tragic consequences of failure to administer the priesthood according to the instructions of the Lord. Leviticus 24:10–23 narrates the consequences of blasphemy of God's name in the camp.

### *Leviticus 8–10: Life and Death in the Presence of God*

To this point in the narrative neither the priesthood nor the cult has been exercised in Israel. Exodus 28–29 describes the priestly garments and ordination procedure, but neither ordination nor properly instructed worship led by an ordained priesthood is found in Exodus; only the non-prescribed cult of the golden calf. The prescriptions for sacrifice are revealed only after the divine indwelling in Israel's midst is complete. Sinai's covenant and building instruction and God's indwelling precede sacrificial prescription, priestly ordination, and the beginning of Israel's cult. Worship and priesthood are rooted in Sinai; Sinai shapes them, not they Sinai. Death follows failure to heed this instruction. This is the function of Leviticus 8–10 within the overarching narrative.[13]

---

13. Watts distinguishes between "interposed narrative," Exodus 32–34 and Leviticus 8–10, and "floating narratives," Leviticus 24:10–23. Floating narratives "lack all temporal connections with the overarching narrative." Watts, *Reading Law*, 87.

In compliance with the instructions of Exodus 29, Leviticus 8 narrates the consecration of the tabernacle and Aaron and his sons. Their consecration converges: apart from the consecrated space of the tent the priesthood cannot function; without a properly consecrated priesthood the tent stands idle. Thus the ordination takes place at the entrance to the tent of meeting (8:4, 31, 33, 35) where the community gathers (8:3–4), and where Aaron and his sons must remain for seven days.

The tabernacle and the Aaronic priesthood are consecrated with scrupulous attention to the divine instructions, as indicated by seven-fold repetition of the execution formula "just as the LORD commanded" (8:4, 9, 13, 17, 21, 29, 36). Failure to consecrate and administer the cult according to authorized norms occasions death (8:35). By their ordination Aaron and his sons stand at the intersection between God and his people, between the clean and the unclean, the holy and the unholy, between the order consequent upon conformity to divine instruction in the camp and the chaos that characterizes disobedience and life outside of God's presence. Without Aaron and his sons unclean Israel has no life in God's presence. With this consecration Israel's cult may officially begin in God's gracious and dangerous presence.

On the eighth day Aaron and his sons, because they have been elevated to the priestly status, begin their ministry at the entrance to the tent (9:5). They exercise their authority not to maintain their own status as a priestly elite but to enable the Lord's appearing to Israel (9:4, 6, 23, 24; r'h "to see," "appear"). When all is done in accordance with divine instruction the Lord "appeared to all people. Fire came out of the presence of the LORD . . . and when all the people saw it, they shouted for joy and fell face down" (Lev. 9:23–24). They did not see God himself (nor did Moses, Ex. 33:20, but see Num. 12), but got as close to God as Moses at the bush (Ex. 3:1–6), and almost as close as Adam and Eve in the garden. Assembling in God's presence according to his instructions, under authorized cultic leadership, brings great joy to God's people, a joy in sharp contrast to the pleasure of the golden calf liturgy (Ex. 32:17). In the nature and character of the priesthood the fundamental problem of uncleanness in the presence of God has been addressed. But it has not been solved; there remains a problem: the priesthood itself.

Because they work in God's presence priests must be scrupulously clean. Thus special regulations attach to them for food, marriage, the death of a friend, or for the High Priest the death of his father or mother (Lev. 21:1–15); a bodily defect renders them ineffective for ministry (21:16–24). Designated sacred offerings may be eaten by the priest and his family, but no unauthorized person may eat from them (22:10–16; see v. 13b, *zr*, "unauthorized"). Finally the priest must keep all of God requirements, including the sacrifices (22:17–33; cf. Mal. 1:10–14), or he will "die for treating them with contempt" (22:9). The priesthood is an exacting and dangerous vocation; it may be exercised only in humble submission to liturgical authority. This Nadab and Abihu did not do; they "offered unauthorized [*zr*] fire" (10:1; cf. 22:13). By failing to administer the liturgy in "the prescribed way" (9:16), Aaron's sons demonstrate contempt for God's voice, for the instructions that bring life into the space shaped by God's presence. Thus they die. They would not be the last: the reactionary Levites Korah, Dathan, Abiram, and many of their followers were swallowed by the earth (Num. 16:31; the sons of Eli, 1 Sam. 2:12–17, 22–25).

The narrative interposed between the sacrificial and cleanliness instructions narrates the authentic and authorized cult by which

Israel maintains its identity and life in God's presence under priestly guidance and authority. The brief narrative of Aaron's corrupt sons warns against the threat of breaking the newly formed redemptive relationship, especially by those charged with its maintenance. For priests and people alike, life and death in God's presence depends upon humble submission to divine instruction. According to God's good pleasure, Aaron and his sons would serve, fallibly, until God appointed a priest according to the order of Melchizedek, Jesus Christ who is "holy, blameless, pure, set apart from sinners, . . . who serves . . . in the true tabernacle set up by the Lord, not by man" (Heb. 7:26; 8:2).

### Leviticus 24:10–23: Death for Blasphemy Outside the Camp

The story of the blasphemer clearly fits Watts's category of "floating narrative" for, unlike the ordination account, it is difficult to discern its relationship to the overarching narrative. Like the ordination narrative, however, where Moses and Aaron performed according to God's instructions, the story of the Israelite-Egyptian blasphemer depicts Israel as a community dealing correctly with an "alien" disobedience: "The Israelites did as the LORD commanded Moses." (24:23). This narrative statement of compliance has its companions in Leviticus 16:34b and in those found in Leviticus 8–10. A cursory examination of these texts discloses that these declarations describe compliance in particular spaces: in Leviticus 8–10 to the priesthood's workspace: the tabernacle space; in Leviticus 16 to the unclean space where the scapegoats are sent, outside the camp; in Leviticus 24:10–23 to Israel's workspace: the camp (cf. "Do no work" [23:3, 7, 8, 21, 25, 28, 35, 36; 25:4–5, 11]). This suggests that the spaces God has redemptively created must be administered in accordance with his instructions. Upon the occasion of a defilement not covered by the received instruction, as with Leviticus 24:10–13, Israel must seek a judgment from the Lord[14] at the place where he chooses his Name to dwell. Furthermore, the linking of Leviticus 8–10 and 24:10–23 and the Day of Atonement speech—which begins by recalling the Nadab and Abihu incident—by an instruction-compliance format, suggests that the narrative sections illustrate the consequences of compliance and non-compliance.

**Table 6.2 Compliance and non-compliance narratives**

|  |  |
|---|---|
|  | **Tent of Meeting** |
| Leviticus 8–10 | Instruction for ordination |
|  | **Moses and Aaron obey** |
|  | Nadab and Abihu disobey |
|  | Death of Nadab and Abihu |
|  |  |
|  | **Tent of Meeting and Camp** |
| Leviticus 16 | Scapegoat to be dedicated at the Tabernacle and sent outside the camp for atonement of all sins (16:16) |
|  | **Israel obeys** |
|  |  |
|  | **Camp** |
| Leviticus 24:10–23 | Israelite-Egyptian blasphemes |
|  | Death of Israelite-Egyptian prescribed |
|  | **Israel obeys** |

14. See Watts, *Reading Law*, 87, on this text and the problems faced by the daughters of Zelophehad in Num. 27 and 37.

But the blasphemy narrative is also linked to its nearer context: it interrupts a series of instructions on feasts and their attendant sacrifices, linked by the repetition and combination of the number seven (23:3, 5, 6, 8, 15, 16, 24, 27, 33, 35, 39, 40, 41, 42; 25:4, 8, etc.; 26:7, 28) and the repetition of "Sabbath" (23:3, 11, 15, 16, 32, 38; 24:8; 25:1, 4, 6, 8, etc.; 26:2, 34, 35, 43). Placed where it is, following six instructions about feasts (23:1, 9, 23, 26, 33; 24:1) and immediately before the seventh (25:1),[15] the blasphemer narrative literarily breaks, interrupts, Sabbath instructions, not unlike Israel's golden calf apostasy, also located between two Sabbath references (Ex. 31:12–17; 35:1–3). Both violations lead to the death of the guilty parties, thereby echoing the sentence upon Adam and Eve for having defiled the space God created for his dwelling among them.[16]

The narrative itself is uncomplicated: the blasphemy occurs in the camp, the punishment outside the camp (24:10, 23); the instruction (24:13–16), however, is complicated by the juxtaposition of a reflection on the law of the *talion* (24:17–22). Like the scapegoat on the Day of Atonement the blasphemer will die outside the camp; unlike the scapegoat, he will die for his own sin. The juxtaposition of this law to the instruction concerning the blasphemer forces the reader to evaluate the punishment of death by making comparisons: the death of an animal requires appropriate restitution of an animal and an eye for an eye; no

15. Leaving aside chapter 27, often designated an appendix. The instruction that would be the seventh is separated from the others by the narrative introduction and conclusion (24:10–12, 23). In addition, the instruction responds to a unique case: the blasphemy of an Israelite-Egyptian. The answer is clear: "Whether an alien or native-born, when he blasphemes the Name, he must be put to death" (24:16; cf. 24:22).

16. At the time of the golden calf episode the guilty Israelites are punished *inside* the camp (Ex. 33:27), but then the tabernacle had not yet been built and thus the Lord's presence had not yet come into Israel's camp.

more, no less. Similarly the killing of a human being requires an appropriate restitution: an eye for an eye, a life for a life; no more, no less.

This juxtaposition of narrative and law provides an *a minori ad maius* argument: if the killing of animals requires such and such a restitution, and the murder of a man the life of the murderer, how much more the blasphemy of the Name? But what greater punishment than death can there be? To be put to death outside the camp, to be forced into exile from God like Adam and Eve—no greater punishment than this exists for the adherent of the biblical narrative (Gen. 2:17; 3:23; Luke 16:19–31). For that reason it is important to remember that the scapegoat's death outside the camp covered all sins and uncleanness, including those for which there was no cleansing (Mark 5:25–34; Heb. 13:11–13). Because God walks in their midst (26:12; cf. Deut. 23:12–14 and Gen. 3:8) the people, like the priests, must scrupulously maintain the camp's purity.

## The Structure of Leviticus

Commentators agree that Leviticus is composed of the following sections:

Leviticus 1–7—instructions for sacrifices
Leviticus 8–10—ordination of the priesthood
Leviticus 11–15—instructions for daily cleanliness
Leviticus 16—the Day of Atonement

Leviticus 17–26 have been treated as a single block, the Holiness Code, but this designation depends on the source-critical discussion of the Pentateuch's compositional history. Within these chapters, however, groups of texts may be discerned as follows:

- Leviticus 17: regulations concerning the place of sacrifices and the role of blood in atonement
- Leviticus 18 and 20 listing prohibited relationships which defile; frame chapter 19 on daily holiness.
- Leviticus 21–22: *instructions* for priests, ends with section on unacceptable sacrifices (instruction to all Israel).
- Leviticus 23–24: *instructions* to Israel for cultic festivals and attendant sacrifices. Focus on Sabbaths and days in sevens or multiples thereof.
- Leviticus 25–26: jubilee and land sabbaticals; rewards and punishment (framed by references to Sinai).
- Leviticus 27: regulations for dedicating to and redeeming from the Lord. Ends with reference to Sinai. Often designated as an appendix.

Combining these thematically with the first 16 chapters, Erich Zenger[17] suggests the following outline:

**Table 6.3 Zenger's outline of Leviticus**

| Leviticus | | | | | | |
|---|---|---|---|---|---|---|
| 1–7 | 8–10 | 11–15 | 16–17 | 18–20 | 21–22 | 23–26, 27 |
| Sacrifices | Priests' Ordination | Daily Cleanliness | Reconciliation | Daily Cleanliness | Priests' Instructions | Sacrifices & Feasts |

17. Erich Zenger et al., *Einleitung in das Alte Testament* (Stuttgart: Kohlhammer, 1995), 37.

This analysis has the virtue of integrating chapters 17–26 into the preceding chapters. It also places the central accent of Leviticus on reconciliation to the Lord according to his instructions in the space designed for clean and holy living. Like Leviticus for the entire Pentateuch, so chapters16–17 depict what is fundamentally necessary for true life in God's presence, according to Leviticus.

## Waiting for the Land

Although we can calculate from Exodus 40:17 (first day of the first month of the second year, Passover [Ex. 12:1]) and Numbers 10:11 (the twentieth day of the second month of the second year) that from the assembly of the tabernacle at Sinai to Israel's departure is little more than six weeks, Leviticus betrays no chronological interest. Unlike Exodus and Numbers, Leviticus is atemporal. At Sinai Israel finds herself in the presence of the Creator's earthly throne and therefore at the earthly center of his realm. Furthermore, because at Sinai Israel is as distant from Egypt as she is from Canaan, no culture, ethnicity, or soil defines her. Divine instruction is her culture, her ethnicity, her soil; her past, present, and future (Lev. 18:1–5). In Leviticus Israel finds herself at the dead center of a rite of passage, typically characterized by atemporality and aculturality. This shapes her waiting for the land.

Leviticus represents the climax of the exiles' journey from outside the garden, through Ur and Egypt, to Sinai. It functions as a "time out" in which God prepares his people to enter the land there to embody divine instruction in a redemptively chosen space like the garden of Eden (Gen. 13:10). Without the instructions of Leviticus, Israel's life before God has no chance of survival, no direction. She has been separated from the nations to receive the special instruction to live among the nations as God's special people (Lev. 15:31; 20:26, "to separate," or "to set apart").

Leviticus not only explains in detail the meaning of Exodus 19:5–6, but also God's primary instruction and promise to Abraham (Gen. 12:1–3): priestly instruction blesses Israel and shapes her to be a blessing among the nations. Bound to God by covenant in Exodus, she is shaped by him to be his own in Leviticus. Without Leviticus, Israel would be just another among many nations in Canaan; she embodies divine instruction in God's presence as does no other people. With this in mind we can understand Leviticus' references to the land. Waiting for the land means acknowledging the need for special instruction to embody God's will in the land. Thus Leviticus inculcates patience for God's people on their journey to the land and a new realism about its value.

Even though the narrative depicts Israel in the desert, Leviticus reminds the reader that the Lord requires loyalty in the land (e.g., 18–20; 25–27) promised to Abraham. Nevertheless, the land itself—the spiritual shape it has by virtue of the religious ways of its non-Israelite inhabitants (18:24–30; 20:22–26)—may not instruct Israel. As with the camp in the desert, God instructs his people to fill the space he has redemptively granted them in Canaan with a ritual and moral life that conforms to the Lord's decrees alone (18:1–5). Neither the desert nor the land itself is the goal of Israel's aspirations; the separation from Egypt achieved by moving into the desert must continue in Canaan (11:45; 20:26). The goal set before Israel is to "follow (hlk) my decrees and . . . be careful to obey my commands" (26:3). If Israel achieves this goal "the LORD will walk (hlk) among you and be your God"

(26:12). But if Israel turns hostile toward (*hlk 'm*, 26:21) the Lord, he himself will be hostile to her (*hlk 'm*, 26:23, 28) and the people will become hostages in the land of their enemies (26:38, 39; but see 26:40–45).

Leviticus prohibits the land from shaping Israel in any way because it is not the goal of Israel's journey with God, even after they receive it as an inheritance. The promise of divine presence is fundamental for Israel, not the land. Israel would learn this the hard way through Ezekiel's disclosure that the Lord did not need the land to be present with his people in exile (Ezek. 1:1–3); and again when Jesus taught that the temple in Jerusalem would no longer be the instrument of God's dwelling among his people (John 1:14; 2:20–21). The body of Christ, by the power of the Holy Spirit, would embody God's will in his presence. Striving so to do God's will, Hebrews reminds Abraham's descendants through Jesus Christ to "make every effort to enter that rest [which remains], so that no one will fall by following their example of disobedience" (Heb. 4:11).

# 7

## Numbers: The Next Generation—The Priestly Army of the Lord

**Summary.** The Lord instructs Moses to take a census of Israel's army. He continues to instruct Moses that he organize Israel as a military camp and teach the people not to defile his presence. Aaron will bless Israel. After celebrating the Passover, the Lord leads the people from Sinai toward the land. On the way they complain and the Lord gives them quails for meat, but many die. The spies give a bad report about the land so that Israel refuses to enter. God hears and tells the people that they will die in the desert; their children will enter the land. The army defeats Sihon and Og and then reaches Moab, where God blesses Israel, but Israel sins with the Baal of Peor. Moses takes a census of the second generation's army; they will inherit the land. The daughters of Zelophehad receive their father's inheritance. Gad, Reuben, and half the tribe of Manasseh receive their possession and are warned not to repeat their fathers' rebellion. The Lord instructs the daughters of

Zelophehad to marry within their clan to maintain the tribal inheritance. These are the regulations the Lord gave through Moses to Israel on the plains of Moab.

**Central narrative interest.** Through Moses, God leads the second generation of his people toward the Promised Land after the first generation has rebelled against God and died in the desert (Num. 14:26–35).

## Connection with Antecedent Narrative

Although Numbers uses more narrative description than Leviticus, its opening recalls Leviticus 1:1: "The LORD spoke to Moses in the Tent of Meeting," but then adds, "in the Desert of Sinai on the first day of the second month of the second year after the Israelites came out of Egypt. He said: . . ." The Lord's speaking to Moses *in* the Tent, not *from*, provides continuity; the shift in geographical location from the mountain to the desert and the chronological notation assert discontinuity. The reference to the desert links the beginning of Numbers to Exodus 19:1 and the chronological notation to Exodus 40:17, thereby linking itself more to the narrative interests of Exodus and at the same time isolating Leviticus at the mountain in non-chronological narrative time. Nevertheless, Numbers maintains continuity with Leviticus by reference to the Tent, and the subsequent divine instructions to Moses.

The linear narrative sequence also requires that Numbers be read in the context of Leviticus' sacrificial, cleanliness, and holiness instructions. Leviticus has deepened the scope of Israel's covenant commitment so that at the beginning of Numbers she is more fully instructed in God's will than she was in Exodus. For one month now the Lord's fiery presence has been in the camp and Israel has received the instruction for survival in that presence, so that when she moves toward the land, having received the additional instructions in Numbers, Israel is under new constraints. Israel can no longer be agnostic about the shape of life in God's presence; she is accountable as never before. This explains why God's response to Israel's complaints during the transition from the desert of Sinai to the plains of Moab now includes death.

Besides the dates (Num. 1:1; 7:1; 9:1; 10:11; Ex. 40:17), Numbers develops other themes initiated by Exodus: the community as an armed camp, the journey toward the Promised Land, the complaints, fear of the promised future, the opposition of the nations (especially Balak's Pharaoh-like fear of Israel's multitudes), and idolatry; all shaped by divine instruction through Moses. In continuity with Leviticus, Numbers also develops the pentateuchal resolution to the conflict defined in the opening chapters of Genesis: human failure to respond appropriately to divine instruction.

## The Fundamental Problem and Plot Development in Numbers

### *The Problem Defined*

Since plot development depends upon conflict and complications, Numbers[1] presents an unusual challenge because its first ten chapters contain no conflict of any kind; there is no rebellion and no one dies. Israel is unquestioningly obedient to all

---

1. For my work on Numbers I am indebted to Dennis T. Olson, *The Death of the Old and the Birth of the New: The Framework of the Book of Numbers and the Pentateuch* (Chico, CA: Scholars Press, 1985), and more recently his *Numbers*, Interpretation (Louisville: John Knox, 1996).

the instructions she receives from her Sovereign: "The Israelites did all this just as the LORD commanded Moses" (Num. 1:54; 2:34; 3:51; 4:49b; 5:4b; 8:3, 20; 9:5, 23; 10:13). Through the end of Numbers 10, Israel is depicted as an obedient, armed, and priestly community, on its way to the Promised Land, fully instructed to negotiate and survive the problems that the desert or the Lord's enemies may present. And, Numbers 10:33 reminds the reader, they set out from the mountain of the Lord. It is the nature of this community on the move that sets the stage for further plot development in Numbers.

The Lord has organized his armed camp in gradations of holiness: the tabernacle in the center, the Levites around it, and the tribes encamped around the tabernacle at some distance from it (2:2, 17). The Levites are placed between the Tent and Israel to guard the people against divine wrath (1:53). There follow prohibitions against approaching the sanctuary (3:10; 4:17–20); there is potential for defiling God's presence (5:1–4); uncleanness may interrupt the good order of the camp (6:9–12; 9:1–14). This potential for problems, an undertone[2] in a narrative that depicts a compliant people, is rooted in the Lord's presence among his people.

Israel's remarkable obedience changes dramatically in chapter 11. Without warning or defining the specific problem, the narrative shifts to Israel's complaints "in the hearing of the LORD." Equally suddenly, "fire from the LORD burned among them and consumed some of the outskirts of the camp." Ever since the conclusion of Exodus the fire of God's presence has been in

---

2. Olson argues for an interplay or dialogue between two voices in chapters 1–10: a dominant voice of obedience and order with an underlying voice of danger and death. *Numbers*, 8, 59. Similarly in Num. 11–25, where the dominant voice is of death and disorder "mixed with whispers of hope for a new generation." Chapters 26–36 are "positive and hopeful. But the reader also hears lingering threats and warnings." *Numbers*, 8, 192–93.

Israel's midst in the tabernacle (Ex. 25:8–9; 40:34–35). Before that it provided light on her way out of Egypt, and now on her way through the desert (Num. 9:15–16). But it is also a "consuming fire" (Ex. 24:17; cf. Heb. 12:29). When God first appeared to Moses the fire did not consume the bush (Ex. 3:2), but it scorched Egypt (Ex. 9:23–24, "lightning" ['š]; cf. 14:24). At the beginning of Israel's official cult, fire from the presence of the Lord consumed the burnt offering, to Israel's joy (Lev. 9:24); from the same presence it consumed Nadab and Abihu for their unauthorized sacrifice (Lev. 10:2). The potential danger of this theophanic fire, indicated in Exodus (3:2; 24:17) and realized among the priesthood in Leviticus (10:1–3), now becomes a deadly reality for God's people in Numbers 11:1–3. Later it will consume Korah's co-conspirators (Num. 16:35). The emergence of this potent symbol in the abrupt juxtaposition of complaint to consistent compliance in the previous chapters indicates the conflict that shapes Numbers: Israel's conduct in the presence of a gracious but dangerous Suzerain.

That God punishes Israel at *this point* in the narrative is crucial for understanding the narrative problem of Numbers for two reasons. First, because Israel has been uniquely instructed the Lord's responses to Israel's complaints increase in intensity. Where in Exodus he had come close to destroying Israel (Ex. 32:10; 33:5), in Numbers Israel's disobedience leads to the death of an entire generation. The event at the edge of the camp is the first indication in Numbers of a shift in narrative situation, one anticipated by Nadab and Abihu's fiery end in Leviticus. Both the priests and the people are now close to God (cf. Lev. 10:3), so close the priests must guard against the deadly divinity for the people's sake (Num. 1:53). The new theological situation, God dwelling in Israel's midst, changes the narrative. Death by fire follows upon failure to hear the sacrificial, cleanliness, and holiness instructions of the Lord. Second, this event is the first of the desert journey depicted in Numbers. Even as the Marah event (Ex. 15:22–27) set the stage for the desert journey from Egypt to Sinai in Exodus, so death at the edge of camp defines the journey from the mountain to the plains of Moab. The deadly conflict between God and his people in Numbers 11:1–3 is not the result of the desert conditions, however; Israel herself is the problem. The narrative expresses this conflict by juxtaposing the chapters of disobedience and death in Numbers 11–25 to the opening chapters of compliance in Numbers 1–10.

### The Problem Developed

If the consuming fire of Numbers 11:1–3 points to a deadly conflict without specifics, the subsequent narrative defines it concretely. The familiar complaints about food and Moses' difficulties in administering the people's needs (cf. Ex. 15:22–17:7; 18) in Numbers 11:4–35 are followed by Miriam and Aaron's opposition to Moses' leadership and Israel's unwillingness to enter the land (Num. 12–14).[3] Although all these affect the journey to the land, it is Israel's unwillingness that compromises it and forms the basis for the fundamental conflict of Numbers.

Where chapters 1–10 describe the arrangement and scrupulous obedience of the Lord's army, Numbers 13–14 depicts an army guilty of treason. The treason consists in a bad report the spies spread among the Israelites, especially the language used to explain the problem: "We can't attack those people, *they are*

---

3. The Lord's speech to Moses in Numbers 15 isolates chapters 11–14 from the leadership struggles between Korah, his associates, and Moses and Aaron, suggesting that this narrative section should be considered by itself.

*stronger than we are"* (13:31, *hzq hw' mmnw*). This phrase recalls Pharaoh's fearful description of Israel: "the Israelites have become much too numerous for us" (Ex. 1:9, *rb w'swm mmnw*), and anticipates Balak's fear: "they are too powerful for me" (*ky 'swm hw' mmny*, 22:6). The spies' words identify them with significant opponents of Israel's journey to the land such that they convert themselves into obstacles to receiving the promised inheritance. And they fear the land's inhabitants more than God in their midst. "The land we explored," they said, "devours those living in it" (14:32). In their eyes "the devouring land" (*'rs 'klt*) is deadlier than the "devouring fire" that is God in their midst (Ex. 24:17, *'š 'klt*).

Neither Egypt nor the Promised Land are truly dangerous for Israel, God is. He is more dangerous than Egypt and the nations. God's instructions distinguish Israel from the nations; trust in him and submission to his voice will keep them alive (Lev. 18:5). But the spies tempt Israel to fear the land and its inhabitants. Confidence in the Lord's word spoken at Sinai— "I will send my terror ahead of you, . . . I will make all your enemies turn their backs and run" (Ex. 23:27)—is absent. The spies' leadership is so successful that the whole assembly begins to grumble against Moses and Aaron: "If only we had died in Egypt! Or in this desert!" (14:2). Treasonous Israel sides with her new leadership and fears the challenges of the Promised Land, not her gracious but dangerous God.

Israel's unwillingness to enter the land unleashes a conflict with God. As in 11:1–3, the Lord has heard Israel's complaint (14:27) and he responds ironically by granting the people their wish: "I will do to you the very things I heard you say: In this desert your bodies will fall—everyone of you twenty years old or more who was counted in the census and who has grumbled against me . . . as for your children that you said would be taken as plunder, I will bring them in to enjoy the land" (14:29, 31; cf. Rom. 1:24, 26, 28: "Therefore God gave them over in the sinful desires . . . to shameful lusts . . . to a depraved mind."). The spy story also reaches back to the census in chapter 1: though counted ready for war, the Lord's army fails. Repeated readings of Numbers cannot escape this shadow. Though depicted as scrupulously compliant in Numbers 1–10, Israel is by nature a treasonous army and an unclean priestly nation. The spy story sets the tension between the Israel of chapters 1–10 and that of the following chapters by depicting the first generation's wandering through the desert and its shameful end in the apostasy at Baal Peor (Num. 25), after Balak's failed attempt to curse Israel (Num. 22–24). In chapter 25, as in 13–14, Israel is poised to enter the land; and again, as in 13–14 so in chapter 25, the first generation replays its treason.[4] The first generation's wanderings fittingly conclude with a massive execution by plague. And, like 13–14 it is punctuated by a priest faithful to the Lord: this time, Phinehas. Finally, when chapter 26 describes the census of the second generation, it recalls the past problems, especially the treason of the first generation (26:63–65).

### The First and Second Generations

The first generation's rejection of the Promised Land and the divine judgment on them constitutes the major conflict of the plot of Numbers. From that point on death hangs over the first generation: death as the consequence of their wish to die in the desert, death for intentional disregard of the Sabbath (15:32–36), death as the result of Korah and his colleagues' rebellion against Moses and Aaron (16:49), Miriam and Aaron's deaths for their rebellion (20:1, 22–29), death from venomous snakes (21:4–9), massive death as the consequence of Israel's apostasy by worship-

4. Olson, *Numbers*, 152.

ing the Baal of Peor (25:1–18). From 11:1 through chapter 25 the first generation suffers the power of God's anger, first aroused by their complaints in 11:3 (*wyḥr 'pw*) and finally turned away by Phinehas's zeal for the Lord's honor (25:3, 11: *wyḥr 'p yhwh; hšyb 't-ḥmty m'l yśr'l*; cf. 32:13).

If the first generation's rebellion constitutes the problem or the narrative deficit, the resolution of the problem, or the cancellation of the deficit is found in the depiction of the second generation's assumption of the first's responsibilities. Phinehas's execution of Zimri and Cozbi represents this before the second census. Similarly, the second generation responds to the Lord's command to take vengeance on Midian for the Baal of Peor affair. Here the Israelite army fights the Lord's enemies without fear and exterminates them. All soldiers who have killed in battle must be purified and stay out of the camp for seven days for shed blood may not defile the place of the Lord's dwelling (31:19–20; cf. 35:33–34). Moreover, not one of the soldiers went missing (Num. 31:49). Later, the trans-Jordan tribes promise to join the others in their battle for the land; the others do not discourage them as did the first generation (32:16–22; cf. 32:6–13). *Pars pro toto* these trans-Jordan tribes represent the second generation's willingness to move forward without complaint. This is also true for Joshua and his assumption of Moses' position. The anti-Moses movement failed to unseat the Lawgiver; but like the rest of the first generation, Moses' own rebellion does; the great servant of God himself will be denied entry into the promised future. Moses does not pick his successor, nor does Joshua put himself forward (unlike Aaron, Miriam, Korah, and his co-conspirators).[5] Above

---

5. Contrary to contemporary practices, those selected as leaders in the biblical narrative are not noted for calling attention to themselves; self-abasement is a more apt description and perhaps requirement. See, for example, the study by George W. Coats, "Self-Abasement and Insult Formulas," *JBL* 89 (1970): 14–26. In a letter to his bishops, Gregory the Great, addressing the problem of simony, advises them on the selection of candidates for leadership as follows: "Moreover, as one who refuses

all, Joshua will not be a Moses; he receives only a portion of Moses' authority and the Lord's word will come to him through Eleazar the priest, not face to face from the Lord himself (Num. 27:18–21).

The second generation's willingness resolves the problem of the first's rebellion, but it does not bring them into the land; in Numbers they remain on the plains of Moab where they arrived with their parents. Will Israel ever get to the land? Although Israel does not enter the land until the book of Joshua, the tone in Numbers is positive, even during the debacle with the spies in which the Lord's instructions indicate that Israel will enter (Num. 15:2, 18). After the second census, the narrative shifts from the theme of battle to one of inheritance, not just in the census itself (26:52–62), but especially in the stories about Zelophehad's daughters which frame Numbers 27–36.[6] The second generation of Israel will enter the land, but carries along the burden and challenge of its experience of the first generation's response to the Lord (Num. 26:64–65; 32:6–15). "By the end of Numbers, the holy camp of God's people is set to continue its march toward the Promised Land with the warnings of the past and the promises of the future in a dynamic dialogue of warning and promise."[7]

## The Structure of Numbers

Critical readings have concluded that Numbers contains too many disparate pieces and too many genres for it to have a discernible shape. Nevertheless, Bible scholarship has recognized

---

when invited and flies when sought should be brought up to the sacred altar, so one that sues of his own accord and pushes himself forward importunately should without doubt be repelled." In his "Epistle CVI," *Nicene and Post-Nicene Fathers*, Second Series, Volume XIII (Grand Rapids, Eerdmans, 1956), 24.

6. See below, note 11.
7. Olson, *Numbers*, 8.

a generally tripartite scheme based loosely on the geography of Numbers: the depicted events and speeches taking place in and around Sinai, Kadesh, and the plains of Moab. Thus, for example, the following have been suggested:

**Table 7.1 Numbers' tripartite scheme**

| 1:1 | 10:10/10:36/9:15 | Sinai |
|---|---|---|
| 10:11/11:1/9:15 | 21:9/20:13/25:18 | Kadesh/travel |
| 21:10/20:14/26:1 | 36:13 | Moab |

There is little agreement about where these sections begin and end. Nevertheless, the narrative of the journey from "the mountain of God," where God instructed Israel in the camp's organization, to the Plains of Moab opposite Jericho, where Israel shamefully belittled her blessing and vocation under the Baal of Peor, suggests that these events have an abiding relevance for God's people. With this journey in mind, some have suggested two "bridge sections" within a five-part organization.[8]

**Table 7.2 Narrative bridges in the desert of Numbers**

| 1:1–10:10 | | In the Sinai Desert |
|---|---|---|
| | 10:11–12:16 | From Sinai to Kadesh |
| 13:1–19:22 | | Forty years wandering near Kadesh |
| | 20:1–22:1 | From Kadesh to the Plains of Moab |
| 22:2–36:13 | | In the Plains of Moab |

8. Gordon J. Wenham, *Numbers: An Introduction and Commentary*, TOTC (Downers Grove, IL: Inter-Varsity, 1981); Timothy R. Ashley, *The Book of Numbers*, NICOT (Grand Rapids: Eerdmans, 1993).

This refinement underscores the importance of the journey, maintains an essentially three-part organization, and places the consequences for Israel's rebellion in the center. But it does not move beyond a geographically determined organization, nor does it answer who is moving from one place to another, or why Israel wandered forty years in desert places.

The census reports in Numbers 1 and 26 define two groups at the center of Numbers' narrative interest: the generation of Israel that left Egypt, and their descendants, the second generation. The first initiates the conflict with God by disobeying his instruction; the second is instructed that it will escape such conflict and its consequences only by scrupulous compliance with divine instruction. The first generation's conflict with God creates the fundamental narrative interest in Numbers; the potential for similar conflict and its consequences in the second generation challenges all subsequent generations of God's people not to repeat the sins of those rescued from Egypt. In this manner Numbers not only depicts the Israel taken out of Egypt as participating in the Pentateuch's definition of the fundamental human problem defined in the opening chapters of Genesis—failure to submit to the divine voice in his presence—but it also engages the "next generation," the generations of readers to come, in the resolution of that problem.

These census reports also help to understand Numbers' structure: each opens one panel of a literary triptych. Numbers 1–10 describes what God's people are: an armed camp under divine instruction under Mosaic and priestly leadership, with an undertone of potential conflict. It ends with their first journey away from the mountain of the Lord, guided by the cloud of the Lord's presence. The third panel, Numbers 26:1–36:13, begins with a census of the second generation followed by instructions and reminders that it not repeat the sins of the first. The panel in between, Numbers 11:1–25:13, describes Israel winning some battles, but it is generally negative in that it recounts the first generation's disobedience to divine instruction, the deadly consequences, and a series of challenges to divinely appointed leadership.

The Balaam stories illustrate God's power to bless Israel's scrupulous compliance. And where Balaam fails in attempting to bring curses on the people, Israel itself is successful: she brings upon herself the kinds of consequences Balak could only wish for. In a final paroxysm of sexual and cultic apostasy, anticipating the apostasy of the later generations in the land, Israel bowed down before the gods of Moab, specifically the Baal of Peor. Juxtaposed to this narrative of disobedience and death, the third panel's challenge to the next generation is unmistakable.

**Table 7.3 Numbers' structure: A literary triptych**

| 1:10–10:36 | 11:1–25:13 | 26:1–36:13 |
|---|---|---|
| Compliant, armed, and priestly community | Treasonous army and unclean priestly community | Armed, priestly community, challenged to be compliant |
| First generation | First generation | Second generation |

A literary frame composed of two narratives about the daughters of Zelophehad (27:8–11; 36:1–13) defines the boundaries of the third panel, links it to the problems defined and developed in the second—the first-generation Zelophehad has died in the desert and has no sons—and raises a new issue. How will Israel decide on matters not covered by legislation provided in the desert? In the case of Zelophehad: Who will keep his name alive to receive the inheritance? Whom may his daughters marry? In both cases the Lord (27:5; 36:5) instructs Moses, who then conveys God's will, thereby suggesting that the next generation will live by the traditions already received at Sinai and that new problems require disclosures from the Lord. The next generation may not develop its own solutions, but should seek compliance to the Lord's will at all times and in all places. Only such resolute compliance will keep Israel away from wandering in desert places.

Numbers ends with a narrative comment—"These are the commands and regulations the Lord gave through Moses to the Israelites on the plains of Moab by the Jordan across from Jericho" (Num. 36:13)—which evokes the ending of Leviticus: "These are the decrees, the laws and the regulations that the LORD established on Mount Sinai between himself and the Israelites through Moses" (Lev. 26:46; cf. 7:38–39; 27:34). The location has changed, but divine instruction and Moses' unique role as messenger remain crucial. Time and place will change, divine instruction and the messenger through whom Israel receives it do not, until he comes whose "star will come out of Jacob, [whose] scepter will rise out of Israel" (Num. 24:17).

The itineraries of Numbers 10:12; 11:35; 12:16; 20:1a; 20:22; 21:4, 10; 22:1 link two geographic locations: the desert of Sinai (Num. 10:11; the mountain of the LORD, Num. 10:33) and the plains of Moab across from Jericho. In between, encamped Israel moves through desert places and alien lands. By this chain of itinerary notices the narrative moves the reader from the place of instruction where the camp is organized, through desert places and Israel's treason, to Moab, where the first generation commits apostasy and where, through Moses, God exhorts the next generation not to imitate its ancestors.

**Table 7.4 Numbers' itinerary from Sinai to Moab**

| From Desert of Sinai . . . | through the deserts to . . . | Moab . . . |
|---|---|---|
| Compliance of the first generation | Treason of the first generation | Challenge to next generation to comply |

## *The Theological Geography of the Numbers Triptych*

To the three general geographies of Numbers—the Desert of Sinai, the other deserts Israel passes through, and the plains of Moab—must be added the more restricted space of Israel's daily cult and conduct: the camp. Israel is encamped in the desert of Sinai, she passes through the desert places as a camp, and she resides on the plains of Moab in a camp. As in Exodus so in Numbers, geography is theology. In Numbers the geography of the camp attaches uniquely to Israel in the Desert of Sinai and as it moves from there to the plains of Moab across from Jericho.[9]

## *The Desert Camp*

Although the mountain itself is no longer involved in the narrative, its significance is implicit in the phrase "the Desert of Sinai," in noting that Israel moved from "the mountain of the LORD" in 10:33, and by the gradations of holiness that recall Israel encamped around Sinai in Exodus 19 and 24, that shapes the camp itself.

**Table 7.5 Parallels of the tabernacle**

| Exodus | Numbers-Camp | Camp/Tent Complex |
|---|---|---|
| Top of Sinai (24:2, 12) | Tent in middle (2:17) | holy of holies |
| Priests, Levites, elders (24:1, 14) | Levites around tent (1:53) | holy place |
| Israel, at foot of mountain, | Israel, around the tent, | court |
| may not touch it (19:12) | at a distance (2:2) | |

9. The Hebrew noun "camp" occurs approximately 48 times in Numbers (Gen. 7x; Ex. 16x, Lev. 18x, Deut. 9x); the verb "to encamp" 73 times, 42 of those in Num. 33.

The theological significance of the camp arises from its being an analogue of the tabernacle complex. God's presence within the camp consecrates this space and distinguishes it from the desert as clean to unclean. Within this redemptively created consecrated space, divine instruction reinforces Israel's identity as an army (Num. 1–4). Later, whenever the ark moves and the camp follows, Moses will say, "Rise up, O Lord! May your enemies be scattered; may your foes flee before you" (Num. 10:35). This camp, emblematic of God's universal rule over and claims upon all peoples, is the vanguard of God's military campaign begun with Israel in Egypt and consolidated at Sinai (Ex. 15:14–18; Judg. 5:4–11; cf. Ps. 18:7–15). Like Noah's ark before it and the body of Christ later, the desert camp is divinely constructed and instructed space which will safely escort to the promised future those children of Adam and Eve who are Abraham's descendants by faith (Gal. 3:29).

When this redemptively created consecrated camp leaves its place of preparation in the Desert of Sinai, the people, in increasing contact with the nations, will by war and conquest declare the claims of their God. Divine instruction will define every move of this military and priestly camp. But, after leaving, fear and death stalk the camp, and the promised future recedes.

### The Desert Transition: From Life to Death

The desert within which the camp is constructed and through which it moves toward the land is not a mere geographic backdrop for more important events. Desert places represent the opposite of ordered cultivated land and urban areas. Their dryness and infertility inhibit normal human life, their odd creatures have strange habits. No one enters a desert willingly, except perhaps to cross quickly from one habitable place to another.

A desert journey so tests participants that they enter habitable land changed by the experience. In this respect deserts are like rites of passage.[10]

As in Exodus (15:22–18:27), the desert journeys in Numbers (10:11–22:1) move the newly instructed and organized camp from one particular space to another. Through this transition Numbers develops its plot with conflicts and events typical of a liminal zone: rebellion, death, and opportunities for newness. Where in Exodus the desert separates Israel from servitude in Egypt to service in the instructed presence of God at Sinai—a move that includes Israel's complaints and God's unique provisions—Numbers takes Israel from the Desert of Sinai to the border area: the Plains of Moab across from Jericho.

Not the desert's physical challenges but Israel's lack of confidence in the Lord opens the door to the death lurking in the desert. The camp as organized and prepared for the desert journey in Numbers 1–10 is secured for life, but that depends on Israel's compliance. The potential for death is acknowledged in the instructions for cleanliness and holiness: if Israel heeds the voice of the Lord, no desert is too dangerous; if she fails, no fertile land can sustain her (Deut. 8; cf. Matt. 4:1; Mark 1:12; Luke 4:1). The desert transition in Numbers begins with death at the edge of the camp (11:3) and as a result of complaining about food (11:33), to a declaration that the first generation will die in the desert (14:29), and the death by plague on the plains of Moab (25:1–9). The Exodus transition focuses on separation from an enslaved past and moving toward serving a new Overlord. Numbers, expanding on living in the presence of this same gracious but dangerous Lord now in the midst of Israel, depicts the fulfillment of the consuming fire's threat potential

10. As discussed above, chapter 5.

(Ex. 3:2; 24:17): the desert swallows alive all from Israel who oppose the Lord (Num. 16:32), including Aaron and Moses. There is no excuse for rebellion. What can be known about God, the cult and conduct he expects, has been made more clear to Israel at Sinai than to the nations (Ps. 147:19–20; cf. Rom. 1:20; 2:14–15).

As the desert transition in Numbers depicts the consequences of disobedience for the first generation as a warning to the second, so it challenges all subsequent generations of God's people to be compliant on the way to the promised inheritance.

## *Moab, Across from Jericho: The Challenge to Assume the Promised Inheritance*

The plains of Moab are neither desert nor the land of promise, but border country. Like the desert, this space is disordered and chaotic from the perspective of the orderliness of the center, in Numbers, the camp organized by Sinai instruction. Although ultimately subordinate to the center, this space does not yet bend the knee to Israel's Overlord. Only in the future will lands distant from the Sinai-Zion-defined center acknowledge this Lord and willingly shape this space to that Lord's instructions (Isa. 2:3–4; 19:23–25; Matt. 28:19–20; Rev. 21:24).[11] In this still insubordinate space Israel's true identity as a threshold people is affirmed; here first- and second-generation Israel's identities conflict and compete with alien ways of being; here emerges what is true of Israel throughout: effectively called to be God's people and justified by his grace, yet incapable of living out this vocation. Israel is a Janus-faced people. It is then no wonder that

11. See Mario Liverani, "The Ideology of the Assyrian Empire," in *Power and Propaganda. A Symposium on Ancient Empires*, ed. Mogens Trolle Larsen (Copenhagen: Akademisk Forlag, 1979), 306–7, for a brief discussion on the relationship between the imperial center and the periphery.

dangers emerge to challenge this consecrated camp's identity and promised inheritance; Jacob and Israel have experienced such border-crossing threats before (Gen. 32, esp. v. 22; Ex. 14:1–12; cf. Josh. 4:19–24).

The immediate danger arises when Balak hears about Israel's military success against Sihon and Og. Having settled in the land of the Amorites (Num. 21:31, 33), Israel's strength causes Balak to fear them as did Pharaoh before him (22:4–6; cf. Ex. 1:9). To avoid being overwhelmed by the evangelical hosts of the Lord, Balak hires Balaam to curse Israel, but, because the Lord controls Balaam's mouth (Prov. 16:1), Israel survives this spiritual attack to receive blessing upon blessing (Num. 23:11–12; 24:9; Gen. 12:2–3). Balaam and Balak return to their homes; the last attempt of the insubordinate space to foil God's military campaign is a failure.

In the Balak and Balaam affair, Israel was completely passive. In the following event, she becomes active, only to engage in apostasy and so bring on herself the kind of destruction for which Balak had hoped (Num. 25). Israel threatens her identity and promised future in ways unavailable to the nations, eerily anticipating her descendants' apostasy in the Promised Land (2 Kings 17; 23). In Moab Israel behaves like the Moabites, not as God's priestly people. Her apostasy affirms God's earlier judgment that she deserves death in the desert; it also affirms that God's earthly people waver between two opinions (1 Kings 18:20–21). Border space discloses Israel's Janus face, called to obedience, yet profoundly disobedient.

Moses also repeats to the next generation the instructions given to the first generation in the Desert of Sinai, but no longer is this generation to think of itself primarily as an army. This generation is instructed to think of itself as a people about to receive its inheritance, as indicated by a shift in vocabulary from

159

"army" in Numbers 1–25 to "inheritance" in 26–36.[12] Thus, although the next generation will successfully engage in battle (31:1–6), as did their ancestors (Num. 21:1–3, 21–35), they must not forget the humiliating defeat by the Amalekites and Canaanites when the first generation sought to take the land without the Lord's blessing (Num. 14:39–45). Moses instructs the second generation not to repeat the sin of their ancestors (32:14–15). In this way Israel's past disobedience informs the present of the next generation with a view to its receiving the fullness of the inheritance on both sides of the Jordan. Numbers ends by illustrating this with the case of Zelophehad's daughters' future inheritance (36:10–12).

In sum, these aspects of Numbers' geography serve the narrative's theological purposes to describe the redemptively created living space which empowers the priestly army to obedient service, to depict that same community as fatally flawed and capable of survival only under God's faithful blessing, and to challenge that community's next generation to assume loyally the promised inheritance, never to erase from its memory the disobedience of its ancestors.

Numbers works with two generations, but they are the same people of God. With the second generation the narrative introduces the reader to the theological problem of maintaining the identity of God's people throughout the generations. The painful historical experiences embedded in Numbers give no cause for a triumphalist assumption of the promised inheritance. Rather, they provide God's people with a sober challenge to execute their vocation in the light of that memory. In Numbers, it is a

12. The noun "inheritance" (hb. *nḥlh*) occurs 7x in Num. 1–25 and 38x in Num. 26–36; the noun "army" (hb. *ṣb'*) 57x in 1–25 and 16x in 26–36. This clustering suggests that the themes are part of the entire narrative, but have their specific emphases with respect to one or another of the two generations.

Janus-faced people that awaits entry into the Promised Land on the Plains of Moab across from Jericho.

## Waiting for the Land

Neither Egypt nor Moab define Israel's future, but neither will the Promised Land. The desert transition, begun in Exodus and whose end Israel awaits in Numbers, proclaims that her present and future are tied up with the God who spoke at Sinai, and whose presence is uniquely definitive for Israel's identity, for her conduct and cult. Divine presence subordinates geography (Ezek. 1:1–3; Matt. 1:23; John 1:14), indeed overcomes it, as Numbers demonstrates: Israel survives the uninhabitable desert by submission to divine instruction. Within the camp there is life; without, death. This desert camp anticipates life in the Promised Land, indeed is the paradigm for true life, as Numbers 5:3 and 35:34 indicate:

> Send away from the camp anyone who has an infectious skin disease or discharge of any kind, or who is ceremonially unclean . . . so they will not *defile their camp, where I dwell among them.* (5:2–3)

> Bloodshed pollutes the land . . . Do not *defile the land* where you live and *where I dwell*, for I, the LORD, *dwell among the Israelites.* (35:33–34)

The unchanging common feature is God's presence; a second, and different, feature is the locus of that presence: the camp in the desert and the land among the nations. Defilement of that camp results in exile (cf. Gen. 3:23) to an unclean existence in the desert; Israel's defilement of the land would beget exile (2 Kings 17:20; 23:27; 24:3, 20). Numbers teaches Israel that the land she is awaiting is but an expansion of the desert camp; the reasons for and character of life will not change, the journey will only come to a restful end. Deuteronomy 8 will later charge the next generation to live in the land as if it were the desert. If the past failures of the first generation define the future challenge of the next generation, so the present challenge of the next generation in the desert camp anticipates the future life in the land: Get used to living with God in the desert camp and you can live with God in the land. If you repeat the failure of the first generation, you will never enter into your rest (Ps. 95:7d–11; Heb. 4:1–11). The discipline of the desert camp, declares Numbers, is a foretaste and earnest of the promised future in a secure and secured place. Life in the body of Christ is no different. There, too, the divine presence is primary, the geographical location of cult and conduct secondary. Numbers invites God's people forever to think of its life in the land as defined by the desert camp.

The desert camp of Numbers is also in transition—from the Desert of Sinai through desert places to the Plains of Moab—a transition shaped by the tension between obedience and disobedience (Num. 1–10; 11–25) and increasing contact with the nations, as it moves toward the promised future. Israel's waiting in transition discloses opportunities for compliant conduct and cult and the reality of failed spiritual discipline. It is a disciplined waiting, tempered by rebellion, grief, and death; joy and wholesome spirituality are scarce.

Recalling this transition to a "second generation" generations later, Psalm 95 admonishes readers, "Today, if you hear his voice, do not harden your hearts . . . ," reminding them that the Numbers transition has not yet come to an end, that the rebellion of the first generation is forever a challenge to the next generation's cult and conduct in the presence of God. This would be true for the exiles and the returned exiles shortly after the rebuilding of the temple, and for those still awaiting the promised future in Jesus' day; it remains true for the body of Christ scattered among the nations (James 1:1). Aspects of the promised future may change in the biblical narration of this future—the adjustments that made possible Zelophehad's daughters' inheritance, the post-exilic shrinking of the inheritance to the holy city (Neh. 11:1), the collapsing of the land and the city into Christ's tabernacling among his people. But these changes did not emerge from new insight gained by God's people. Special revelation disclosed new shapes or greater fullness of earlier spiritual realities: from the mountain to a camp and cloud, from them to a land and a temple, and from these to the body of Christ and the Spirit. As were the former, so the latter have not yet emerged from the transition of the desert camp.

This transition is also characterized by waiting in border country. In this space the tension between the two generations is clearest because the next generation's memory is forever imprinted with the failure of the first. On the Plains of Moab across from Jericho, waiting Israel is forever the Janus-faced people of God. From chapter 26, however, Numbers illuminates the compliant face by repeating the instructions and shifting its focus to the promised inheritance, especially in the frame stories about Zelophehad's daughters. No one receives the inheritance yet, not even Reuben, Gad, and Manasseh (Num. 32). Along with the rest of the people the trans-Jordan tribes must wait to enter into the fullness of the promise. Past sinful reality and instruction for present and future compliance define Israel's spiritual discipline in the desert camp at the front door of the Promised Land.

The eschatology of Numbers drives Psalm 95:8, 10: "Today, if you hear his voice, do not harden your hearts as you did at Meriba, as you did that day at Massah in the desert, . . . so I declared on oath in my anger, 'They shall never enter my rest.'" This eschatology may be diagramed as follows:

**Table 7.6 The eschatology of Numbers**

| Past | Present (*today*, Ps. 95) | Future |
|------|---------------------------|--------|
| Desert | Camp (Plains of Moab) | Land |
| Time in the land | Exile | Land again |
| Exile | Post-Exile | The Holy City (Neh.) |
| Desert/Land/Exile/ Holy City | Church in the dispersion | New Jerusalem |

Hebrews 3–4 speaks the same truth in the new historical-redemptive situation: the author calls upon the generation of his day to assume the future of the promise in the light of the past of God's people and the divine response to it. Thus all the generations of God's people are called upon to await the promised inheritance by remembering the past of the first generation so that they comply with God's instructions, in his presence, "today."

# 8

## Deuteronomy: Moses' Torah—When You Take Possession of the Land

**Summary.** In the fortieth year of their wanderings, Moses instructs Israel in the torah, teaching the people of God's land promises to the patriarchs, the consequences of the spies' bad reports, and that he himself is not allowed to enter the land because of God's anger. He reminds the people to love the Lord with all their heart, to teach their children the law of God, not to intermarry with the nations or worship other gods. Israel should remember the Lord did not destroy them after the golden calf. Israel must worship at the place the Lord chooses for his name to dwell, to keep all the law of God. When they get to the land they must recite the curses on Mt. Ebal, the blessings on Mt. Gerizim. God will bless Israel if they keep the law; curse them if they do not. The Lord makes a covenant with Israel in Moab. Moses teaches them to read the law every seven years so their children will fear the Lord. Moses prepares for his death, pronounces a blessing upon the tribes, and lays his hands upon Joshua, his successor. After Moses sees the land promised to the patriarchs, he dies. There is no prophet like Moses.

**Central narrative interest.** Moses instructs the second generation to keep the law upon entry into the land so that they may receive the blessings and not the curses of the covenant (Deut. 32:44–47).

## Connection with Antecedent Narrative

There is no obvious narrative continuity between Deuteronomy and Numbers; it begins simply, "These are the words of Moses . . . ," not "the LORD said to Moses," as in Leviticus and Numbers. Deuteronomy's instructions foreground Moses, not the Lord. However, the geographical location of these speeches, the person of Moses, and framing references to the patriarchal land promises (1:8; 34:4) and Moses' death (1:37; 34:5–8) make it possible to hear Deuteronomy as the conclusion of the Pentateuch's address of the narrative problem identified by Genesis.

Geographical references link Deuteronomy to Numbers. The introduction (1:1–5) and conclusion (34:1–12) place Moses' speeches, his death, and the transfer of leadership to Joshua in the Plains of Moab across from Jericho during the fortieth year—the end of Israel's wanderings as the result of her rebellion (1:3; cf. Num. 14:34), just after the defeat of Sihon and Og (1:4; cf. Num. 21:21–35). The historical rehearsal in the opening chapters suggests that Deuteronomy addresses the second generation.

The person of Moses links Deuteronomy to Numbers and more broadly to the antecedent narrative where, except for the Lord, Moses is the leading figure from Exodus on. Except for brief narrations, the words of Deuteronomy belong to Moses, who addresses Israel without receiving instructions from the Lord. Thus Deuteronomy emphasizes Moses' unique authority—God spoke to him as to no other (Num. 12:7–8)—and exalts him above all messengers in the Old Testament (Deut. 34:10). Israel's pilgrimage from Egypt to the border country in Moab is shaped uniquely by Moses (not Abraham); no one else disclosed the will of the Lord to Israel as did he. As such Moses anticipates Jesus Christ, who would reveal God as neither Moses nor Abraham could.

Moses' instructions to the generation awaiting its future are also framed by references to the patriarchal land promises (1:8; 34:4): "This is the land I promised on oath to Abraham, Isaac, and Jacob when I said, 'I will give it to your descendants.' I have let you see it with your eyes, but you will not cross over into it" (Deut. 34:4). These words recall the whole complex of patriarchal promises, especially the initial divine speech to Abraham. God's allowing Moses to see (r'h) the land recalls the Lord's instruction to Abraham in Genesis 12:1: "Leave your country, your people and your father's household and go to the land I will show you ("cause to see" [r'h])." The greatest prophet of the Old Testament will not receive the land as his inheritance. Like the patriarchs, he will die in hope of the promise.

The greatest prophet of the Old Testament also compromised his own future in the land (Num. 20:12). He would be the last of the first generation to die outside the Promised Land. Repeated references to Moses' death (Deut. 1:37; 3:26–28; 4:21, 25; 31:14, 29; 32:14–52; 33:1; 34:5–8) evoke the rebellions of Numbers. His impending death (31:2, 14, 16, 27, 29) recalls the first generation's death in the desert (Num. 14:29–35). Thus Deuteronomy reflects the concerns of Numbers' treatment of the first and second generations. Although Moses himself will die outside the land, his words accompany the second generation into the land. Moses' instructions will lead God's people in the future, as Joshua 1 explains.

## Connection with Subsequent Narrative

According to Joshua 1:7–8 ("Be careful to obey all the law my servant Moses gave you . . . do not let this book of the law depart from your mouth"), Deuteronomy is definitive for Joshua's leadership of the "next generation" in the land. Framing within clusters of the word "law" ("torah") in Joshua (1:7–8; 8:31–32 [trt mšh], 34; 22:5; 23:6 [trt mšh]; 24:26) and 2 Kings (10:31; 14:6 [trt mšh]; 17:13, 34, 37; 21:8; 22:8; 23:24–25 [trt mšh]) argues that this is the case, as do the language and theology throughout Deuteronomy. Life in the land depends on the inscripturated voice of Moses.

The Lord instructs Joshua to obey "the law my servant Moses gave you," and not to "let this Book of the Law depart from your mouth" (Josh. 1: 7–8); just before his own death Joshua similarly instructs Israel to "obey all that is written in the Book of the Law of Moses" (Joshua 23:6). This theme appears repeatedly throughout Joshua–Kings; messengers and prophets remind Israel and her kings of their commitment to "this law." Failure to heed "this law" ultimately brings about Israel's expulsion from the land (Judges 2:1–5; 1 Sam. 2:27; 2 Sam. 12:1–14; 2 Kings 17:7–23; 21:1–15; 23:26–27). The conclusion to Kings depicts the Lord removing Israel from his presence (2 Kings 24:3, 20), as he expelled Adam and Eve long before. Deuteronomy also instructs Israel to worship the Lord alone and not to serve other gods (Deut. 6:1–11:32, esp. 6:4–9), to worship him only at the places he chooses to let his name dwell (Deut. 12; 15:20; 16:2); and not to follow the practices of the nations (Deut. 7; 12). Only by submitting to the voice of Moses, "this law," will Israel enjoy the Lord's blessing (Deut. 28:1–14) and not bend under his curse (28:15–68). The voice of Moses is the norm by which the Lord of all the earth judges Israel's cult and conduct in the land.

In sum, Deuteronomy plays a dual role: it concludes the Pentateuch and provides a critical point of departure from which to evaluate Israel's management of the land.[1] As a conclusion to the Pentateuch it recalls the Lord's dealings with Abraham, Isaac, and Jacob (Deut. 1:8; 34:4) and addresses their descendants who are about to enter the land in partial fulfillment of the Lord's promise (Gen. 12:7). As a vantage point from which to read Joshua–Kings, it instructs Israel how to retain and manage its inheritance throughout the generations.

---

1. For more on the relationship of Deuteronomy to Joshua–Kings, together identified as the Deuteronomistic History (DH), see J. Gordon McConville, *Grace in the End: A Study in Deuteronomic Theology* (Grand Rapids: Zondervan, 1993), and Richard D. Nelson, *The Historical Books* (Nashville: Abingdon, 1998), 67–78. Nelson states the plot of the DH as: "Will Israel continue in obedience to the law of Moses and prosper, or will the people disobey and suffer the Lord's wrath?" See also, "Joshua–Kings and Theories of Deuteronomistic Historiography," in Philip E. Satterthwaite and J. Gordon McConville, *Exploring the Old Testament: A Guide to the Historical Books*, vol. 2 (Downer's Grove, IL: InterVarsity, 2007), 199–219. For a historical-compositional view of Deuteronomy as the ending of the Pentateuch, see Joseph Blenkinsopp, *The Pentateuch: An Introduction to the First Five Books of the Bible* (New York: Doubleday, 1992), 229–32.

**Table 8.1 Relation of the Pentateuch to Joshua–Kings**

| | ← Conclusion |
|---|---|
| Genesis–Numbers + Deuteronomy | Joshua–Kings |
| | Introductory → perspectives |

## *The Homiletical Structure of Deuteronomy*

Unlike Numbers, Deuteronomy uses little narrative; like Leviticus, its genre mixture within a narrative frame depicts movement, the weight of the Mosaic speeches pointing to a homiletical interest in the consequences of obedience and disobedience in the land.

Moses' instruction represents the Pentateuch's concluding contribution to its resolution of the fundamental conflict, the need for divine instruction in God's presence. Deuteronomy forms a second and authoritative recitation of "this law" ("this torah" [*htrh hz't*]: 1:5; 4:44 [*z't htwrh*]; 17:18, 19; 27:3, 8, 26; 28:58; 29:29; 31:9, 11, 12, 13, 24; 32:46, "this Book of the Law"; 28:61; 30:10; 31:26) by which Israel will serve the Lord in his presence. Moses himself will not enter the Promised Land, but the Torah of Moses will; he is textually present. Abraham and Moses pass away, but torah is forever (cf. Matt. 24:35). Only by the torah of Moses will Joshua and Israel enjoy life in God's presence in the land of promise (Josh. 1:7–8; 23:6).

The person of Moses is equally important for understanding the dynamic within Deuteronomy itself. Although the book has no narrative or geographical development like Numbers, Moses' instructions form a rhetoric of persuasion,[2]

---

2. James W. Watts, *Reading Law: The Rhetorical Shaping of the Pentateuch*, The Biblical Seminar 59 (Sheffield: Sheffield Academic Press, 1999), 55–57. On page 57

a homiletical plot bound up with Deuteronomy's further treatment of the generations, the authority of Moses, the transfer of leadership in view of Moses' impending death, and the structure of the book. To develop this we turn first to the structure of Deuteronomy.

### Deuteronomy as Mosaic Instruction and a Suzerain-Vassal Treaty

In Deuteronomy's mixture of narrative, instruction, exhortation, and poetry, the genre of instruction dominates. To answer the question, What unifies this variety of literature? there are two ways of discerning the structure of this material, one focusing on the introductory sentences of major sections within Deuteronomy, another on the organizational elements of international (Hittite or Assyrian) suzerain-vassal treaties. Introductory sentences at Deuteronomy 1:1; 4:44; 29:1; and 33:1 reveal a fourfold division of Deuteronomy.

| | |
|---|---|
| 1:1–4:43 | "These are the words Moses spoke to all Israel." |
| 4:44–28:68 | "This is the law Moses set before the Israelites." |
| 29:1–32:52 | "These are the terms of the covenant the LORD commanded Moses." |
| 33:1–34:12 | "This is the blessing that Moses the man of God pronounced." |

Watts writes: "Deuteronomy obliges Israel not only to legal obedience but also to repetition of the book's own rhetoric of persuasion through reenactment, both by individuals (6.20–25) and by the nation as a whole (11.29; 27.12; cf. 31.10–13). . . . The rhetoric of Deuteronomy employs the elements of story, list and divine sanction more obviously than any other part of the Pentateuch, but it also integrates their effects more thoroughly."

Following these introductions Deuteronomy presents a historical rehearsal of Israel's desert journey from the time of Jethro's involvement, moves to Moses' torah instruction for conduct and cult in the land, then to an additional covenant in Moab with a view to loyalty in the land, and concludes with Moses' final acts. These introductory sentences foreground Moses, not God, as the primary speaker. When God speaks, he does so only to Moses, and then about his death (32:48–52; 34:4).

It has also been suggested that the formal elements of ancient suzerain-vassal treaties lend unity to Deuteronomy. These elements are as follows.[3]

**Table 8.2 Elements of suzerain-vassal treaties**

| | |
|---|---|
| Introduction of speaker | introduction of the suzerain |
| Historical prologue | the beneficial actions of the suzerain, to motivate loyalty of the vassal |
| Stipulations | obligations of the vassal to the suzerain |
| Document clause | requirements for periodic public reading |
| Invocation of witnesses | usually deities |
| Blessings and curses | consequences of obedience or disobedience |

With these elements Deuteronomy becomes "a literary account of the renewal of the covenant on the plains of Moab. The literary (treaty) pattern may be more than merely a literary device; it is probable that it reflects also the ceremony during

3. John H. Walton, *Ancient Israelite Literature in Its Cultural Context: A Survey of Parallels between Biblical and Ancient Near Eastern Texts* (Grand Rapids: Zondervan, 1989), 99–107.

which the covenant was renewed and a successor to Moses was appointed."[4] When applied to Deuteronomy the following structures are suggested:

**Table 8.3 Suzerain-vassal treaties and the structure of Deuteronomy**

| | | |
|---|---|---|
| Introduction | 1:1–5 | |
| Historical prologue | 1:6–4:49 | |
| General stipulations | 5–11 | |
| Specific stipulations | 12–26 | |
| Document clauses | 27:1–10; 31:9–29 | |
| Blessings/curses | 27–28 | 27:12–26; 28 |
| Witnesses | 30:19; 31:19; 32:1–43 | 32:15* |

\* Column one is from Craigie, *Deuteronomy*, 24; the differences in column two are from J. G. McConville, *Deuteronomy* (Downer's Grove, IL: InterVarsity, 2002), 24.

Differences between second-millennium Hittite and first-millennium Assyrian treaties lead to different treatments of Deuteronomy.[5] Nevertheless, the presence of treaty elements is almost universally accepted.

These two approaches to the structure raise the question: Do we read Deuteronomy as an account of a treaty renewal or as Moses' final instructions? There are several reasons for taking the latter as the primary reading. First, the introductory sentences

4. Peter C. Craigie, *The Book of Deuteronomy*, NICOT (Grand Rapids: Eerdmans, 1976), 24.

5. Especially when linked to its dating. The Hittite treaties have a historical prologue and statement concerning the document. In general, those arguing for a late second- or early first-millennium date avail themselves of the Hittite material (Craigie, *The Book of Deuteronomy*, and Gordon J. McConville); those who argue for a seventh-century provenance, for an Assyrian influence (Patrick D. Miller, *Deuteronomy*, Interpretation [Louisville: John Knox, 1990]).

call attention to Moses as the main speaker: "the words of Moses" (1:1), the laws of Moses (4:44), the covenant of Moses (29:1), and the blessing of Moses (32:1). In Exodus through Numbers, God instructs Moses to speak. In Deuteronomy Moses speaks on his own authority.

Second, the elements of a treaty form are recognizable and in their proper order through chapter 28, but it is hardly surprising to find them in the report of speeches recalling the Sinai covenant. Exodus 19–24 also uses treaty elements in its report of a treaty-making event. Deuteronomy is not such a report, but a series of Mosaic speeches whose order reflects aspects of a treaty. But only to a point, for the form cannot account for chapters 29–34. These chapters bring to a climax a theme begun in Exodus, emphasized in Numbers, and underscored in Deuteronomy's authoritative speaker: the exaltation of Moses (Deut. 34:10).

Third, the death of the testator is not an element in the treaty form, but Moses' impending death is crucial to the message of Deuteronomy. It frames Deuteronomy and reminds Israel that even the great man of God failed; Moses' historical acts were insufficient to secure the promise of land. Much more, however, does it continue the depiction of another side to Moses: the most humble man (Num. 12:3; cf. Ex. 3:11; 4:1–17), who submitted to the Lord in all things. For this reason also Deuteronomy can end saying: "Since then no prophet has arisen like Moses"—not until Jesus the Christ. Moses is the Old Testament servant of God who is the closest pre-figurement of Christ.

For these reasons the relationship between the two discerned structures is best expressed by the suggestion that Deuteronomy has an explicit literary structure expressed in the Mosaic speeches, a substructure "discernible in the covenantal character of the Book," and a theological structure focused on "exclusive worship of the Lord" in the place he has chosen.[6] This integrates Mosaic homiletics and covenant polity, with a strong nod to the centrality of Moses. By evoking the covenant Moses mediated at Sinai, the covenant substructure reminds Israel of the bond between them and God, thereby reinforcing Moses' instructions. Because he speaks on his own without divine instruction, even making a covenant between God and Israel in his own name— "I am making this covenant, with its oath, not only with you who are standing here with us today in the presence of the LORD our God but also with those who are not here today" (Deut. 29:14–15)—Deuteronomy depicts a Moses so exalted, with such authority, that his words—the "law of Moses"—not the "law of God," will rule Israel's life in the land.

## The Torah of Moses: A Kerygma of Wisdom for Happy Living in the Land

The kerygmatic character of Deuteronomy is the product of the interplay of history and instruction, instruction undergirded by covenant memory, and the transmission of a normative Mosaic tradition. Together these create a rhetoric of persuasion recognizable as Israel's wisdom (Deut. 4:6).

### History and Instruction

Moses' first speech reviews the history of God's dealing with Israel since leaving Sinai on the twentieth day of the second month of the second year after leaving Egypt (Num. 10:11). The speech rehearses Israel's travel from Horeb—her rebellion

---

6. Miller, *Deuteronomy*, 10–16; and see Dennis T. Olson, *Deuteronomy and the Death of Moses: A Theological Reading* (Minneapolis: Augsburg Fortress, 1994), 3.

after the spies' report; the judgment that the first generation, including Moses, would die in the desert; their wanderings for forty years; the defeat of the kings of Heshbon and Bashan; the division of the land; and a repetition of the Lord's decision not to let Moses enter the land—with a view to inducing Israel to submit to the law he is about to proclaim. That is, a rehearsal of history is followed by the ethical and moral implications of that rehearsal.

This is clear from Deuteronomy 4:1 where the rehearsal shifts to an exhortation ("Hear now, O Israel, the decrees and laws I am about to teach you. Follow them so that you may live and may go in and take possession of the land that the LORD, the God of your fathers, is giving you."), whose adverb "now"[7] introduces the conclusions that should follow the antecedent rehearsal of the past. History is rehearsed with a view to these conclusions. Thus what stands out in Deuteronomy's rehearsal is the first generation's rebellion and its punishment. Like the miraculous signs and wonders in Egypt, this history of God's deeds with Israel serves "so that you might know that the LORD is God and besides him there is no other" (Deut. 4:35; cf. Ex. 19:4), so that Israel may fear the Lord and serve him alone. God's past acts and speech are recalled in the present of Moab with a view to a future in the land shaped by God's instructions and Israel's faithfulness to them.

Moses' second speech (4:44ff) also derives its motivational force from the previous rehearsal of history and goes on to recall God's awesome self-disclosure declaration of covenant instructions. Addressing the second generation as if it were the first

7. The conjunction "now" ('th) typically occurs at the point in historical rehearsals where the audience is prompted to accept the ethical consequences in the present of the past acts of God in relationship with his people. See Joshua 24:14; 1 Sam. 12:16; Neh. 9:32.

(5:2–5), Moses repeats the Decalogue and then expounds the first commandment's absolute requirement of loyalty to the God who delivered Israel (Deut. 6–11). These and the rest of the Mosaic instruction are interspersed with historical rehearsals pointing to God's mighty acts (Egypt, 6:20; 10:19; 15:15; 24:22; the desert, 8:1–5; Moab, 23:5; Amalek, 25:17–19) and rebellions spoken of as if the second generation had committed them ("you [pl.]," 9:7–10:11; 11:5–7). These mini-rehearsals have the same purpose as the historical prologue of a suzerain-vassal treaty: they motivate the vassal to loyalty and create fear of transgressing the stipulations. Moses then moves to the implications of first-commandment loyalty: restricted worship practices, no worship at the place of Israel's own choice (12), and a reinforcement of the prohibition against being servants of other gods (13).

Deuteronomy 6:20–25 is a good example of the move from history to ethical injunction for torah living in the land.

**Table 8.4 Deuteronomic catechesis**

| Question | 6:20 | "What is the meaning of these stipulations?" |
|---|---|---|
| **Answer** | 6:21–25 | |
| | *History* | 21–23: "We were slaves . . . , the LORD brought us to . . . the land that he promised on oath to our ancestors." |
| | *Instructions* | 24–25: "The LORD commanded us . . . that we might prosper; it will be our righteousness." |

Remembering the mighty deeds of the Lord in Egypt and since Egypt in the desert at Sinai and subsequently is crucial for the second generation, who saw their elders die in the desert for rebellion, that they may respond loyally in the land of promise, and also teach their children.

All this from the mouth of Moses.

### Instruction and Covenant

Even as the past mighty acts of God reinforce Mosaic instruction, so the covenant substructure constantly reminds the audience that Sinai and its covenant are the great historical event and motive for loyal service in the Lord. Its impact is heightened when Moses tells the second generation that "it was not with our fathers that the LORD made this covenant, but with us, with all of us who are alive this day" (Deut. 5:3) because this links the covenant directly to the second generation who experienced the death of the first generation as the result of that generation's covenant disloyalty. Although Moses speaks, the underlying authority is the covenant at Sinai. Moses' second set of instructions, already motivated by references to history, is reinforced by covenant curses, which Israel will pronounce upon herself (Deut. 27), and the consequences of obedience and disobedience.

The oath-bound polity of Sinai and the rehearsals of history combine to form a persuasive argument for loyalty in the land. These elements are further reinforced with a covenant made in Moab. But it is a covenant made "in Moses," with Moses taking God's place: "I am making this covenant, with its oath, not only with you who are standing here with us today in the presence of the LORD our God but also with those who are not here today" (29:15; Acts 2:38). As Moses stands in for God, so the second generation stands in for all the subsequent generations of God's people.

Moses' reference to the covenant oath here and his earlier instruction about vows in Deuteronomy 23:21–23 underscore the seriousness of the covenant substructure of Moses' instruction.

In this rhetoric of persuasion Mosaic instruction is reinforced by historical acts of deliverance, sustenance, and punishment, memories of the theophanic fire (4:33, 36), and the oath-bound relationship established at Sinai.

## Transmission of the Mosaic Instruction

Death will not be an obstacle to good life in the land. Moses will die without entering the land, but his death will not annul his authority nor abrogate his instruction. Joshua will lead Israel into Canaan, yet Joshua is not Moses but his servant (Josh. 1:1) who received only some of his authority (Num. 27:20). Consequently, Joshua will not lead Israel according to his own vision, but according to "the law my servant Moses gave you; do not turn from it to the right or to the left, that you may be successful wherever you go. . . . Meditate on it day and night" (Josh. 1:7–8; Deut. 31:1–8). Before his death Joshua passes this instruction on to the people: "Be careful to obey all that is written in the Book of the Law of Moses, without turning aside to the right or to the left" (23:6). God's words to Joshua also recall Moses' teaching concerning Israel's royal leadership (Deut. 17:14–30).

**Table 8.5 Parallels between kingship and leadership instruction**

| The king | Joshua |
|---|---|
| read this law (17:19) | meditate on the law (1:8) |
| all the days of his life (17:19) | day and night (1:8) |
| not turn from the law to right or left (17:20) | not turn from the law to right or left (1:7) |

These parallels, the later description of King Josiah's reign—he did not turn to the right or to the left, but served the Lord "with all his heart and with all his soul and with all his strength, in accordance with the law of Moses " (2 Kings 22:2; 23:25)—and the framing of Joshua–Kings by torah clusters (see above), indicate that Moses' instructions are normative for life in the land for the people and their leadership, but especially for the kings. The kings' failure to submit to Mosaic leadership eventually leads to Israel's exile.

Good life in the land depends upon delight in the law of the Lord and daily meditation on it, as Psalm 1 declares. This is the responsibility of kings and the people: "Happy is the man who . . . meditates [on the law of the Lord] day and night." Such happy people prosper (Josh. 1:8) and stand upright in the Lord's judgment. The wicked, who do not delight in the law of the Lord, have no such future. Meditating on the law sinks roots deeply into the source of the law, the Lord himself, and *that* brings a harvest of happiness. Not the land, but the Lord himself is Israel's heritage.

The Levites will maintain the authority of Mosaic instruction by reading it every seven years so the people "can listen and learn to fear the LORD your God and follow carefully all the words of this law. Their children, who do not know this law, must hear it and learn to fear the LORD your God as long as you live in the land you are crossing the Jordan to possess" (Deut. 31:12–13). And the fear of the Lord is the beginning of wisdom.

### Instruction and Wisdom

The people of Israel learned to fear the Lord when they saw Egypt lying dead on the shore of the sea through which they themselves had passed on dry ground; then they began to trust God's servant Moses (Ex. 14:31). At the end of their journey, in the boundary land on the plains of Moab, Moses instructs

Israel to fear the Lord through "this law," a mixture of history, instruction, and covenant. The fear of the Lord inculcated by "this law" will demonstrate Israel's wisdom and understanding among the nations (Deut. 4:6).

"This law" will guide Israel and its leaders in distinguishing between wisdom and folly when confronted by the "other gods" and their worshipers in the land. The people failed in this and were exiled (2 Kings 17:16–20; 21:9; 23:26–27). "This law" would also lead kings to accept Lady Wisdom's invitation (1 Kings 3:10–14; 4:29–34; 10:6; Prov. 9:1–6; 8:15–16); failure to heed "this law" will bring them to fall for Lady Folly's enticements (1 Kings 11:1–13; Prov. 9:13–18). Keeping the law, counsels Proverbs 7:1–5, keeps one from the arms of the strange woman (1 Kings 11:1; and see Prov. 5:10, 20).

Moses himself exercised torah wisdom when he selected helpers to deal with the people's needs and difficulties (Deut. 1:13; Ex. 18:13–27). His reward was a long life (Prov. 16:31; 19:23; 22:4), ten years more than the Egyptian ideal of 110 which Joseph enjoyed. Love of "this law" (Pss. 19:7; 111:10; 112) produces a wisdom the nations can only envy, but which can be Israel's through the fear of the Lord, as it was for Rahab (Josh. 2:9). The practice of Moses' law will demonstrate a wisdom that the nations will desire in order to save themselves from the destruction that their folly will bring on them (Zech. 8:23). Israel's foolish refusal of this gift will land her in exile until she practices the wisdom that comes from God through a prophet greater than Moses (1 Cor. 1:18–2:5).

## Waiting for the Land at the Threshold

Deuteronomy is a boundary book. Geographically it keeps Israel on the Plains of Moab where Mosaic instructions hedge her in between a rebellious past and a landed future, between a past of God's acts of salvation and sustenance and a future of oath-bound service surrounded by the temptations of the nations still in the land. Literarily, Deuteronomy concludes the Pentateuch without entry into the land—one of the major promises to Abraham—and with the death of Moses, who has led the people from death in Egypt to life at Sinai, and from death in the desert to a hopeful future in the Promised Land, if rooted in faithful submission to Mosaic instruction.

Geographically, God's people are closer to the land, and, in Moses, can taste her full redemption. Nevertheless, Deuteronomy refuses to surrender the gift: land remains a tantalizing promise. Deuteronomy fully instructs God's people to root life in God's presence and his instructions, so that they may be ready when they are called to cross the Jordan. As such, Deuteronomy calls upon God's people to be a boundary people, one dwelling in the threshold to the promised future, one awaiting the promised future as a people whose identity is not measured by property but by rooting herself in "this law" of Moses like a plant beside streams of flowing water.

God's promise to Abraham, "Go to the land I *will* show you" (Gen. 12:1), maintains its future character: Moses has seen it, Israel will see it. Thus Moses often says, "when the LORD your God brings you into the land" (6:10; 7:1; cf. 17:14; 18:9; 26:1; etc.). The Lord also tells him about "the land I am giving you" (i.e., Israel, 9:6; 32:49, 52), disclosing that the gift of land is an ongoing process, one that is about to become a reality. Finally, we read that the Lord "has given" the land (1:21; 3:18) indicating completion. Together these form an eschatology of land: the gift is irrevocably given, but it remains in the almost-to-be-realized future. That is, Deuteronomy declares to all who have ears to hear it: God's people own no territory. In its canonical form Deuteronomy spoke thus to the generations who lived in the land, in Egyptian or Babylonian exile, and in Jerusalem after the exile. By the end of the Old Testament, the land itself disappears from view; all that remains for Israel's hope is the holy city, Jerusalem.

Deuteronomy speaks similarly to the "twelve tribes scattered among the nations" (James 1:1; cf. 1 Peter 1:1), who are still waiting the fullness of the promise (Heb. 4:1–11), and the fullness of God's glory when he comes to dwell with his people in the new Jerusalem (Rev. 21). God's people remain a boundary people, without a place to rest their heads, *until.*

Moses' death also contributes to Deuteronomy's view of waiting for the land. As the closing event of the Pentateuch, the theme of Moses' death outside the land evokes the curse of death that accompanied Adam and Eve in their exile from the presence of God. Moses may have died outside of the land, but not in exile from the presence of God. Because God himself buried Moses after the great leader saw the land, Moses was buried in hope, and his death stands in continuity with those of the patriarchs, who died in hope of the Promised Land, indicated by their burial in Machpelah.

But Moses was not buried in Machpelah, the grave particular to the patriarchs, in which Joseph would yet be buried. In death, Moses' life was hidden "in God" (cf. Col. 3:3); it would not be defined with the grave particular to the patriarchs. His bones could not be found to be transported to the family plot. Moses' unique death outside the land evokes that of Enoch, who walked with God in the exile from Eden and "was no more, because God took him away" (Gen. 5:24). Moses' death outside the land evokes the death in exile of all the non-Abrahamic children of Adam and Eve; it suggests, before Israel even enters, that death outside the particular land is not a fundamental problem but that death outside of "this law" is.

Moses' voice, embedded in Deuteronomy as "this torah," will accompany Israel into the land; torah is completed outside the land, and is complete without the land. But it accompanies Israel into the land as the ongoing voice of Moses for all the generations to live in the land as not yet having received it (Deut. 8). In the land Israel's life will be covenantally bound to God "in Moses." As part of that torah, the account of Moses' death outside the land relativizes the importance of land and teaches that death and burial in the land are not necessary, but that dying in the Lord is. Moses' death foreshadows one who would die outside the city for all Adam and Eve's descendants, both Jew and Gentile.

# 9

## Waiting for the Land Today: The Church as a Desert People

I n their never-ending search for security and food, people have squabbled over and gone to war to defend or take land. At the beginning of the twenty-first century, such struggles continue between Pakistan and India, Tibet and China, indigenous peoples in the Americas and the colonizers, and among the tribes throughout Africa. International borders too are being challenged by the poor, oppressed, and unemployed. Who has a right to keep these people from working in another land?

No matter whether we think about land as a private possession or tribal property, local or even international law has seldom stood in the way of land grabbing by war, simple theft, squatting, or sophisticated "legal" maneuvers. Land is the ultimate prize in humanity's search for the good life, because, it is widely believed, land is the source of life.

185

The Pentateuch disputes this belief. Its opening chapters declare that God is the source of life and land, that without him there is neither life nor land. This is uniquely true of humanity. God created Adam, Eve, and their descendants to live in his life-giving presence, a presence that makes any land, anywhere, a good place to live. God himself is the source of life. Being in his presence so deeply satisfies our needs that it provides good and long life anywhere. But Adam and Eve's descendants are engaged in a never-ending flight from God's presence, an enforced wandering from Eden and ill-considered Babel. In this flight humanity is not without land, for the nations have received their inheritance from the Father of all (Deut. 32:8). But they are without God, for he exiled them from his life-giving presence.

In this enforced wandering humanity turns the gift of land into a problem: a created thing becomes divine, the source of life (Rom. 1:25). Exchanging the truth for a lie, humanity no longer honors the Creator of all. Like the older prodigal son (Luke 15:28–32), we refuse to acknowledge God himself as the source of life. Among Adam's descendants, only Israel receives the Lord himself as an inheritance (Deut. 32:9). At the end of the Pentateuch, Moses reminds Israel and the subsequent genera-tions of God's people of what has been true since the exile from Eden: that life on the land away from God's presence is only just bearable (Gen. 3:17–19); that the abundant life is available only in God's presence; that her life was hidden with God, through Moses, in the desert (Deut. 8:3–6; Col. 3:3).

Ending with Israel at the edge of the Promised Land and barely out of the desert, the Pentateuch declares that Israel's unique identity is not rooted in her pilgrimage toward the land, for all peoples seek such rest; neither is it defined by possessing a piece of the land, for all claim some tie to the land where they live; nor in being a resident alien, as was Abraham, for no one is at home in this world. Rather, it is the gift of being brought into God's terrifying presence (Deut. 4:32–40) that distinguishes God's people from the nations. Having called Israel out of her oppressive past in Egypt God enticed his people into his desert presence by mighty works, there to await his appearance and his leading of her through and beyond the Jordan.

The land of promise remains a future reality throughout the Pentateuch; between Egypt and Canaan the divine presence becomes a present reality. For this reason the desert, not the Promised Land, emerges as the crucial theological geography for Israel's identity. Life in the desert presence of God is primary, not the Promised Land. How does that primacy shape our understanding of waiting for the land today? To answer that question we will briefly examine two views that emphasize the primacy of land and a third that moves toward the primacy of presence. The latter view will be developed in concert with the Pentateuch's theology of the desert as foundational for the church's waiting for the land today.

## The Primacy of Land

Classic dispensationalism holds that ancient biblical promises to the patriarchs entitle the modern state of Israel to live in the Promised Land. It holds that the Old Testament promises do not have in view the Gentile church but physical Israel, and that prophecy must be literally fulfilled for and by that Israel. By virtue of the Palestinian covenant[1] the land promised to

1. "The Palestinian Covenant gives the conditions under which Israel entered the land of promise. It is important to see that the nation has never as yet taken the land under the unconditional Abrahamic Covenant, . . . nor has it ever possessed the whole land." Note to Deut. 30:3 in *Oxford NIV Scofield Study Bible* (1967).

the patriarchs belongs uniquely to physical Israel, its future
tied to a new temple in the physical land of promise. John F.
Walvoord writes:

> Dispensational interpretation holds that the term Israel is never
> inclusive of Gentile Christians and that while both enjoy the
> same privileges in the church in the present age, . . . in the
> present age, Jew and Gentile can become one in Christ without
> losing their racial or national characteristics. In the future the
> distinction between the Jew and Gentile will again become
> more distinct as Israel receives special blessings in the millen-
> nial kingdom, whereas Gentiles receive other blessings during
> the same period. Even in the new heavens and the new earth
> the ethnic distinctions continue, though all believers share the
> same blessings.[2]

The connection between the Old Testament land promise
for physical Israel and the return of Christ which signals its
fulfillment leads Christians committed to this theological position to support modern Israel's claims to the land. Moreover,
because Jewish resettlement of the land since 1948 is viewed
as a fulfillment of Old Testament prophecy, this position also
disputes Palestinian claims to the land. Waiting for this land to
become fully Israel's requires prayer and preaching, and conduct

---

2. John F. Walvoord, "Does the Church Fulfill Israel's Program?" in John F.
Walvoord and Roy B. Zuck, eds., *The Bib Sac Reader: Commemorating Fifty Years
of Publication by Dallas Theological Seminary, 1934–1983* (Chicago: Moody, 1983),
49–50. The war with Iraq in the early 1990s was the occasion of Walvoord's *Major
Bible Prophecies: 37 Crucial Prophecies That Affect You Today* (Grand Rapids: Zondervan,
1991). This book became a bestseller, as was his *Armageddon, Oil and the Middle East
Crisis: What the Bible Says about the Future of the Middle East and the End of Western
Civilization* (with John E. Walvoord; Grand Rapids: Zondervan, 1974) during the
oil crisis in the early 1970s. For a critical discussion of classic dispensationalism, see
Hans K. LaRondelle, *The Israel of God in Prophecy: Principles of Prophetic Interpretation* (Berrien Springs, MI: Andrews University Press, 1983).

focused on bringing about the reality promised by the Palestinian covenant, including the socio-economic transformation of a specific geography. In this view, waiting for the land means helping the modern state of Israel hold on to its land so that one day it may enjoy God's presence in that land, and so that, ultimately, faithful Gentile Christians may be blessed with God's presence in heaven.

Others hold that the Old Testament's speech about the conquest of ancient Canaan covers up an original revolution during which non-Israelite peasants overthrew foreign oppressors to establish an egalitarian society. Tribes who escaped slavery in Egypt joined this revolution and lent it their name, "Israel," and that of their God, YHWH. This new egalitarian community became "biblical" Israel. Some centuries later, Philistine aggression required a military leadership which brought about the end of this social revolution, ironically, by developing a royalist social order similar to one their ancestors had overthrown centuries before. The kingship described in the canonical text, according to this theory, developed from this royalist counterrevolution.

Because the canonical Bible tells the story written by royalists to justify their reassignment of land ownership,[3] testimony to this "biblical" Israel can only be recovered by critical socio-historical reconstruction of "biblical" Israel. This reconstructed Israel was composed of a Canaanite peasantry and a few Israelite tribes who together established an egalitarian society. The canonical Bible, however, tells another story: imperialist Israel

---

3. The classic formulation of this position is Norman K. Gottwald, *The Tribes of Yahweh: A Sociology of the Religion of Liberated Israel, 1250–1050 B.C.E.* (Maryknoll: Orbis, 1979). Gottwald goes to some length in the opening chapter to emphasize the anti-idealist (i.e., transcendence) materialist basis of his reconstruction. In general this position is labeled as liberation-theological and is inclusive of those who argue that Scripture supports the liberation of oppressed minorities.

destroys the Canaanite peasants to take their land. Robert Allen Warrior writes:

> If indeed the Canaanites were integral to Israel's early history, the Exodus narratives reflect a situation in which indigenous people put their hope in a god from the outside, were liberated from their oppressors, and then saw their story of oppression revised out of the new nation's history of salvation. They were assimilated into another people's identity and the history of their ancestors came to be regarded as suspect and a danger to the safety of Israel. In short, they were betrayed.[4]

From this viewpoint, the biblical narrative is an account of the betrayal of Canaanite peasants. Accepting the claims of the canonical Bible only continues the betrayal.

Like classic dispensationalism, a materialist-liberationist reading of Scripture also argues that ownership of and rights to the land are primary, but with a significant difference. In the latter view, the oppressed are justified in taking the land from those who dispossessed them, be they the foreigners from whom they salvaged their own land with the help of Israelite tribes, the traitors who subverted the egalitarian revolution and now hold the land as divinely appointed kings, or contemporaries who interpret reality according to the canonical view. The problem, however, is the biblical narrative itself. "Historical knowledge," Warrior writes, "does not change the status of the indigenes in the *narrative* and the theology that grows out of it. . . . History is no longer with us. The narrative remains."[5] The canonical narrative covers up the "dangerous

4. Robert Allen Warrior, "A Native American Perspective: Canaanites, Cowboys, and Indians," in *Voices from the Margin: Interpreting the Bible from the Third World*, ed. R. S. Sugirtharajah (Maryknoll: Orbis, 1991), 294.
5. Ibid., 290.

memory" of the historical struggle for freedom of "biblical" Israel. Only courageous socio-critical exegesis of the canonical text will allow that memory to emerge.

With the product of such a critical deconstruction in hand, Norman K. Gottwald defines the contemporary enemy of egalitarian "biblical" Israel—the military-industrial complex, middle class bourgeoisie commitments, American imperialism, and the built-in conservatism of ecclesiastical establishments—and challenges socially committed Christians today to recognize their solidarity with "biblical" Israel and to unite in a supportive solidarity to establish a counter-society.[6] He writes:

> These are some of the ways we are linked in historic continuity with those who have gone before us, with those mothers and fathers of our faith, those first Israelites. I for one do not intend to surrender these forebears in the faith to the reactionaries in the churches who do nothing but distort and dishonor them. There is a task for socially committed Christians to hold up the mirror of biblical Israel before the churches so that the freshly glimpsed social image out of the past can prompt a new self-appraisal of "social mission"—of what it means to be a self in this society and what it means to be a church! We Christians should deny any easy claim to affinity with those early Israelites, unless we too are willing to hazard our present life toward that fuller human existence that lures us onward in time.[7]

Like "biblical" Israel, socially concerned contemporary Christians should unite in the struggle against oppressors. Properly deconstructed, the biblical narrative is about oppressed people taking charge of their own lives, freeing themselves from

6. Norman K. Gottwald, "The Impact of Ancient Israel on Our Social World," *CurTM* 6, no. 2 (1979): 92.
7. Ibid., 93.

imperialisms of different kinds; it is the story of a minority throwing off the yokes of a bondage by the majority. The egalitarianism that "biblical" Israel achieved long ago is possible today for the poor, women, those of varieties of sexual orientations, and colonialized and indigenous peoples everywhere.

This position rules out life in the presence of God in the traditional theological sense; "God" is only a cipher for the process of social liberation. It also excludes *waiting* for the land; that is the oppressor's way of postponing social justice. The land belongs to those who assume the egalitarian traditions of "biblical" Israel; it is only a question of repossession, of dispossessing the rich, the powerful, the military, and hegemonic sexual and economic practices. There is no waiting, only the struggle for social transformation and a more humane existence now. In this view, the liberated will build the heavenly city on earth today.

Both views argue for Israel's right to the land: Classic dispensationalism for the Israel of the canon as read through Scofield's understanding of prophecy; materialist-liberationists for the "biblical" Israel recovered from the canon's royalist propaganda. The former defends the modern state of Israel; the latter would join the struggle of the dispossessed, such as those who occupied these territories before 1948.

Twentieth-century biblical theology has also lent considerable weight to the primacy of land by arguing for a Hexateuch (Genesis–Joshua) in which the earliest of Israel's confessions connects the exodus with land settlement (Deut. 26:5–9), bypassing the Sinai traditions. Others, arguing from a promise-fulfillment perspective, assert that Genesis' promise to Abraham is fulfilled in Joshua's depiction of Israel's coming to rest in the Promised Land. Both, however, argue that land is the primary goal of Israel's wanderings.

The problem with these approaches is Deuteronomy;[8] without it Joshua and the land settlement would immediately follow upon Numbers. But the canonical Bible lets Israel enter the land only after Deuteronomy's sober reflection on her desert rebellions, her refusal to enter the land, and solemn instruction in "this law" for productive life in the land. The journey, then, ends not with settling the land of Canaan but in waiting for it at the border. Moreover, the Pentateuch also ends with the death of the man who stood in God's presence as none other, a presence that has defined Israel since her arrival at Sinai: Moses. Only with Joshua, servant of Moses, does the time of Israel's dwelling in the land begin.

## Toward a Primacy of Presence

A third view argues that the Promised Land anticipates the fullness of life in God's presence, and that this is centrally fulfilled through Jesus Christ. This fulfillment in Christ argues for a defining role of divine presence in the theology of land, especially since the Old Testament gives definitive shape to the land in terms of the divine presence in the Jerusalem temple. The New Testament's speech about Christ (John 1:14) and the heavenly Jerusalem as redeemed humanity's dwelling in God's presence (Rev. 21) reinforces this. David E. Holwerda writes,

> The New Testament focuses on Jerusalem as the essence of the promise of land, . . . since the conditions for inheriting the land are fulfilled only in Jesus and since he is the temple where God dwells, the New Testament locates the temple where Jesus is. Jesus is in heaven and so is Jerusalem. Claims to citizenship

8. See James A. Sanders, *Torah and Canon* (Philadelphia: Fortress, 1972), 42, 45.

are established by faith in Christ, and hence members of the Church, the body of Christ, are also citizens of that city.[9]

Holwerda's view is open to the mystery of Israel's future role, but the land of promise and earthly Jerusalem as concrete geographic entities, like Noah's ark, the desert tabernacle, and the temple of Solomon, no longer play crucial redemptive roles. Their time is past. The body of Christ, the church (John 2:20; 1 Cor. 3:16–17), wherever it is found (Gal. 6:16; James 1:1), now exercises a central redemptive role. Once the ark saved Noah and his family from death, now Christ secures his people by baptism until the storms of this present age have passed. Similarly, the desert camp was designed to keep Israel safe in God's presence during the journey from Egypt to Canaan; now Christ keeps his people undefiled in their scattered awaiting of the descent of the heavenly Jerusalem on the new earth (1 Peter 3:13; Rev. 21). Only then will there be fullness of life in God's presence.

This view does not argue for the primacy of the land, neither as that promised to Israel nor as that which belongs to the dispossessed of the earth. It does not share classic dispensationalism's interest in the post-1948 state of Israel, nor materialistic-liberationism's commitment to land rights for the dispossessed.[10] Rather, it understands the Promised Land as the space which temporarily provides life in God's presence, a space concentrated in the Jerusalem temple.

---

9. David E. Holwerda, *Jesus and Israel: One Covenant or Two?* (Grand Rapids: Eerdmans, 1995), 111.

10. Although he criticizes the patristic and medieval use of the new covenant, Samuel Terrien's comments in *The Elusive Presence: The Heart of Biblical Theology* (San Francisco: Harper & Row, 1978), 26, apply to positions arguing for the primacy of land: they "confuse eschatological hope with real-estate appropriation, promise with earthly possession, and vocation with presumed prerogative."

Christ's coming has relocated and redefined that space in two ways. First, the body of Christ now is the temple of the Holy Spirit and is composed of Jews and Gentiles who confess Christ as Lord. Together they await the fullness of Christ's presence when he comes in glory. Second, because the divine indwells the body of Christ, all its members have become priests called to be faithful in keeping the temple of God pure and unpolluted from the world (2 Cor. 6:14–7:1; 1 Cor. 3:16–17; 6:18). This is not a new thing for God's people: stewardship of the space consecrated by God's presence became their holy burden at Sinai, in the desert. It was there that God brought Israel into his fiery presence, called them to be a priestly nation (Ex. 19:5), and revealed that he intended to dwell in Israel's midst (Ex. 25:8–9; 29:43–46). In his desert presence God taught Israel how to dwell safely in his presence: by remaining faithful to him and undefiled (Lev. 26:3–13; 14–39), and by not contaminating the land as did the nations before them (Lev. 18:24–28). The desert teaches the primacy of God's presence.

## Israel in God's Desert Presence

Israel's waiting for the land, her future reality, is shaped by the intimate presence of God, a present reality since Sinai. As Sinai became a holy mountain because God descended on it, so Israel became a holy people by the divine indwelling at Sinai. The Lord's fiery presence shapes the narrative from the seventh plague through Numbers; Moses recalls the theophanic fire's impact in Deuteronomy 4:24, 36; 5:22, 24. During Israel's desert journey from Egypt to Canaan (Ex. 15:22-Num. 22:1), the Lord brands himself on her life such that this desert presence becomes formative for her life in the land (Deut. 8). It is a more intense form of Abraham's wandering in God's presence (Gen. 17:1, "before me"). As a whole, then, the Pentateuch declares to God's people of every generation that the presence of God *already* is, but that the land is *not yet*, a present reality. Until the exile is completely resolved by the coming again of Immanuel, God's people will have no place to call home.[11]

By rooting Israel's identity and vocation in the inhospitable desert, the Pentateuch declares it to be Israel's normal earthly home. Forty awe- and terror-filled years in a hostile and infertile desert with the God of their salvation form the theological crucible in which Israel waits for the land. She has no arable land in which to lay down her head (Luke 9:58). The only earthly geography that truly matters to God's people in this world is the desert between Egypt and Canaan.

Focused on life in the tabernacle presence, the desert narrative forms an enduring catechesis in three parts. A pre-Sinai catechesis (Ex. 15:22–18:27) instructs God's people in her separation from the past and a transition to the promised future; a Sinai catechesis instructs her in cult and conduct in God's consuming-fire presence (Ex. 19:1–Num. 10:35); a post-Sinai catechesis teaches about dying to the old life and rising to the new (Num. 11:1–22:1). This narrative triptych depicts three aspects of waiting for the land: an enduring separation and transition,

---

11. The New Testament also emphasizes the present reality of God's presence: "The Hebraic theology of presence provides the structure of the Markan gospel, the culmination of Stephen's sermon, the *self-asseverative* formula ("I am the Lord") in Saul's vision on the Damascus road, Paul's description of the church as the temple of God, the Lukan *legenda* on the Annunciation, the Johannine prologue on the 'word encamped as a tent,' the typology of the epistle to the Hebrews, and the allegory of the new Jerusalem in the book of Revelation. It is the same theology of cultic presence, bringing together in the liturgical present the memory of the *magnalia dei* and the expectation of the day of Yahweh, which undergirds the eucharistic meal of the early church; for the memory of the last supper is bound to the awaiting of the *parousia*." Terrien, *The Elusive Presence*, 30.

an enduring and undefiled cult and conduct, and an enduring dying to the old life and rising to the new.

## Pre-Sinai Catechesis: Enduring Separation and Transition

Israel's exodus from Egypt continues the separation from the nations that her ancestor Abram began. She may still think of Egypt as the source of life (Ex. 16:3), but that world is no longer available. In the post-Egypt desert, Israel learns to assume Abram's single-minded devotion to walk perfectly in the presence of God (Gen. 17:1). Upon reaching Sinai, Israel is as far away from Ur as Ur was from Eden. Conversely, at Sinai she is almost as close to God as were Adam and Eve in the Garden.

In the desert, normal life support is unavailable; creation's resources cannot provide a good living. Uprooted from normal life conditions, Israel must now draw support from a hitherto unknown and totally unmanageable source. Because Egypt no longer sets the table, Israel must learn to depend on a Redeemer she hardly knows. The desert journey to Sinai provides clear hints about the true source of life: the instruction of the Lord (Ex. 15:25–26; 16:4, 16, 24, 28, 32, 34; 18:13, 16, 20–24, 26). Because dependence on divine instruction is so alien to the survival skills learned in Egypt, Israel complains and rebels, activities typical of a transition from the old to the new.

In the transition from what she was in Egypt to what she will become at Sinai, Israel behaves as teenagers do who are moving into adulthood: they "stretch the envelope," complain about the leadership, and rebel against their Redeemer. Celebrating God's salvation at the seashore was almost natural, living with *this* Redeemer alone, learning to know him, letting this unknown

197

deity begin to shape life instead of the vicious but known Pharaoh, compelled Israel to a heretofore unknown discipline. Where the plagues and the sea crossing broke the shackles of Egyptian vassaldom, the desert transition forges a new, but equally encompassing, servitude. The move from traumatic dependence on Egypt to the bitter waters of Marah so disorients the people that they rebel against the new strictures of righteousness. In the desert between Egypt and Sinai, Israel is forever a teenager, bound to a testing of her new status.

God tests his people (Ex. 15:25; 16:4; cf. 20:20; James 1:2–4) to uncover their true identity and intentions, as he did with their ancestor Abraham (Gen. 22:1). Will Israel, like Abraham, submit to God's Word as the source of daily bread? Will she, like Abraham, abandon her known Egyptian past of slavery for the unknown shape of servitude to the Lord? Israel's constant grumbling betrays the depth of her dependence on Egypt. Outside pressure adds to an apparent hopelessness. Although God has destroyed Egypt, Amalek arises to oppose God's way with Israel. They left Egypt an armed camp (Ex. 6:26; 7:4; 12:17, 37, 41, 51; 13:18), but when called upon to fight the Lord's wars in his victory march from Egypt, success comes only through God's chosen servant, Moses (Ex. 17:8–16).

Israel's separation from Egypt and her arduous transition to Sinai depicts Israel's "natural" identity for subsequent generations of God's people, whether newly in the land with Joshua, crying to God in the time of the Judges and Samuel, deep into their worship of other gods during the time of the kings, in Babylonian exile, or in the time of Nehemiah and Ezra. Whenever veteran Israelites and their children hear this desert narrative, they are exhorted to a constant eradication of their Egyptian past and its forms of dependence, and encouraged to dependence on the God of their salvation. Israel's desert transition from Egypt to

Sinai defines how believers at all stages of sanctification wait for the land: not in triumphal transformation of the desert, but in the regular testing of a rebellious heart and the experience of God's surprising provision of daily sustenance.

## Sinai Catechesis: Bound to Worship in God's Presence

Having experienced God's victory over Egypt and the grace of bread and water in the desert (Ex. 19:4), Israel accepts God's offer of covenant at Mt. Sinai (19:5–6, 8; 24:7–8). Binding herself with an oath to Egypt's destroyer signals Israel's willingness to submit her entire existence to this relatively unknown Sovereign. Thus begins the Sinai training in the knowledge of God and servant openness to the new Lord's stipulations for cult and conduct.

### Covenant Instruction in the Face of Divine Terror

Without a formal covenant, Pharaoh treated Israel as his own vassals and forced them to build his own strategic store cities. Some Israelites even identified themselves as Pharaoh's servants (Ex. 5:15–16). In truth, they were descendants of Abraham, with whom God had made a covenant. Pharaoh's arrogant enslavement of Israel led to his destruction and Israel's freedom from Egyptian servitude. By swearing a covenant oath with Egypt's destroyer, Israel formally broke all ties to Pharaoh.

At Sinai God reminds Israel how he delivered them from Egypt, sustained them in the desert, and brought them into his presence (Ex. 19:4). When he offers them a covenant in the context of such kindness, Israel indicates a willingness to accept the conditions (Ex. 19:8). Before the blood oath is concluded, however, God reveals another side: his dangerous power. Israel is enjoined from touching Sinai on pain of death and mighty Sinai trembles (19:12–19; cf. Hab. 3:1–15); mere mortals will die in his close presence (19:12; 24:2). Israel is terrified to death (20:18). Day and night God's consuming-fire glory is visible to Israel (24:17). With true knowledge of God's goodness and his dangerous power, and acceptance of the stipulations of the covenant, Israel swears loyalty with a blood oath (Ex. 24:3–8). They will do all the Lord commands, and worship no other gods (23:20–33).

### Building in the Desert: Cult and Conduct

Having dealt with Egypt's threat to Abraham's descendants and having received Israel's oath of servitude, God instructs the people to begin his own building project: a place for the consuming-fire God to dwell in their midst (Ex. 25:8; 40:34–35). This construction will not transform the desert into arable land to fill Israel's earthly needs, but will provide a place where heaven will invade earth to create a unique space for life in God's presence.

Sacrifices, cleansing rituals, and other cultic activities in the divine presence remind Israel that "I am the LORD their God, who brought them out of Egypt so that I might dwell among them" (Ex. 29:46). As described in Leviticus and Numbers, the cult reinforces the truth that the goal of Israel's march from Egypt is not first of all to enter the Promised Land, but to live cleanly in God's presence, as Adam and Eve once did in the Garden of Eden.

Within the camp, only the holier space of the tabernacle is in perfect order, for God himself dwells there, and only the scrupulously cleansed priesthood may enter it on behalf of Israel. Priests mediate between the perfection of God's presence and the uncleanness that permeates life in the camp. By means of divine instruction they cleanse the camp and banish all uncleanness from it, consigning it to destruction in the desert. Cleansing of the cult and conduct trains Israel for life in the Promised Land, which must be cleansed like the desert camp (Lev. 18:24–30; Num. 35:34). Shaped by divine instruction in God's own presence, Israel foreshadows the body of Christ as the temple of God, in which each member is a living, priestly stone (1 Peter 2:5, 9; cf. Ex. 19:5).

### Leaving Sinai: A Fully Instructed Army

Mt. Sinai has finished its revelatory task; from now on the Lord will speak to his people from the tabernacle. But the Israel leaving Sinai is no longer the shapeless band that arrived there: the Lord has instructed them in the cult and sanctified them by his presence, and divine instruction clearly reshapes them as a military camp (Num. 1–4). Enthroned in the midst of his people, God leads his people toward the Promised Land.

The journey from Sinai continues the military victory march begun on the night of the first Passover, but now there is no fear of the enemy, for all tribes contribute to the army, except for the Levites, who protect Israel from the wrath of the Lord in their midst (Num. 1:53; 2:17). During the march to Canaan, Israel must keep the Lord's camp undefiled (Num. 5:1–4), for only so will this people wholly separated to the Lord receive his blessing on their way (Num. 6:22–27). After the entire community brings its tribute to their sovereign they celebrate the Passover, close ranks, and leave Sinai guided by the glory cloud. Whenever they moved, Moses would say: "Rise up, O LORD!

201

May your enemies be scattered; may your foes flee before you"
(Num. 10:35).

Will Israel encounter other nations on this march from Sinai?
Will she stay centered on the Lord's instruction when that happens? Will she maintain her holiness and separation from the
world around her?

## Post-Sinai Catechesis: Dying and Rising

Death lurks in the desert, waiting to devour the foolish who
reject the means of survival God offers. When intransigent Israel
takes God's presence for granted, the divine fire scorches her
and many suffer a dreadful plague (Num. 11:3, 33). Then, the
generation that experienced God's mighty acts of salvation in
Egypt, praised their Redeemer with abandon at the Sea, lived
by divine sustenance in the desert, and trembled at his terrible
self-disclosure on Sinai, all with a view to receiving the Promised
Land, refuses to enter it for fear of its inhabitants. This first
generation will die in the desert never having received the land
as their inheritance (Num. 14:28).

The journey from Sinai to the plains of Moab turns into
a death march. For 38 years the generation wanders in the
desert; the bush that burned but was not consumed before
Sinai (Ex. 3:3) now is consumed by God's anger: at the edge
of the camp, because of their complaints about food, their
unwillingness to enter the land, the rebellion against Moses
by Aaron and Miriam and Korah and his followers. This Israel
enjoys military success against the king of Arad, and Sihon and
Og, and Moab fails to curse Israel because the Lord turned
Balaam against Balak. However, when Israel indulges in sexual
immorality with Moabite women and worships the Baal of

Peor, she brings upon herself a terrible plague. The generation that escaped death in Egypt and the threat of the Sea, dies in the wilderness, her own worst enemy.

God then repeats his instructions to the children of this first generation. The second generation will not suffer for the sins of their parents; they will enjoy life in the land if they heed the voice of the Lord. Thus Zelophehad's daughters will receive their father's inheritance; his sin will not override the promised future (Num. 27:1–11; 36:1–12). The death of the first generation challenges the second generation to rise to new life by fully heeding the Word of God in their midst.

## The Church-Temple Desert Disciplines

According to the Pentateuch, Israel's life is hidden with God in the desert. The desert is not only an historico-geographical reality but also a theological reality, one that teaches Israel not to think of herself as a landed people, for no earthly soil can produce the fruit of righteousness. The desert journey reminds all generations of God's people that only those roots will bear fruit in season which are watered by divine instruction (Ps. 1:1–3). God's instruction transforms his people in the desert: in his presence the unholy becomes holy and the unclean clean.

The desert of the Pentateuch remains hostile and inhospitable to life; it is not transformed. This desert remains a place of utter dependence on God; of separation from the nations and their "menus" for happy living; of rebellion, disobedience, suffering, and death characteristic of the transition between Egypt and Canaan; of binding, instruction, and organizing this redemptively created space for holy cult and conduct. Only within this camp, sanctified by God's presence in the midst of his people, can these descendants of Abraham enjoy enduring life. Ironically, it is in the desert that Israel finds the only fertile soil capable of producing the bread and water of life: instruction in God's desert presence. But the desert itself remains untransformed.

Life in God's presence is the truth that must sustain Israel in the land; the land itself is not the prize at the end of this journey. In Canaan, Israel must keep the desert instruction for her cult and conduct. God will withhold the rain when Israel follows the cult and conduct of the gods of the land. Such disloyalty defiles the presence of God and renders the land unclean and inhospitable to the divine presence. Thus, Israel's time in the land ends with her exile from God's presence and her banishment to the wilderness of the nations (Ezek. 20:35), which are hostile and inhospitable to life lived by God's instructions, as the books of Esther and Daniel show.

At the beginning of his ministry, Jesus went into the desert and was successful where Israel (Matt. 4:1–17) and Adam (Luke 4:1–13) had failed.[12] The itinerary of his ministry, shaped by total dependence upon the Father's instruction, takes place among the rebellious, complaining, suffering, and dying of God's people; he makes the unclean pure, the unholy whole. When he dies abandoned to a darkness more hostile than any desert, Jesus completes the desert journey for his people. With his ascension he brings them into the intimate presence of God (Heb. 10:19), from where he pours out the Holy Spirit to indwell the body of Christ, the church, God's temple (1 Cor. 3:16; 6:19) on earth.

Thus indwelt, the church of Jesus Christ awaits a promised future: not land to cultivate, but rest from her work just as God rested from his (Heb. 4:6–11), a full rest in God's presence for all who have been cleansed by the blood of the Lamb (Rev. 21).

12. Ulrich W. Mauser, *Christ in the Wilderness: The Wilderness Theme in the Second Gospel and Its Basis in the Biblical Tradition*, SBTh 39 (London: SCM Press, 1963).

The church awaits this future in the desert (Rev. 12:6)—the earth made desolate by the pursuit of the ancient dragon—exercising the disciplines required to survive its hostility and inhospitality by the power of the indwelling Spirit. Thus God's people will cultivate the fruit of the Spirit by exercising the following desert disciplines.

## The Desert Discipline of Separation and Self-Denial

The desert disciplines are those of a threshold people who live between what they were in Egypt and what they will become in the promised future, a people who have no soil of their own to cultivate. Separated from earthly cultures and ethnicities, and in transition to the heavenly city, God's people will suffer a constant uprooting from the soils of their past and will be eager for enduring instruction in righteous cultivation of the fruit that produces holy distraction from the world and its interests.

From Abraham to Ruth, and from David to Jesus Christ, this separation forms the church's fundamental identity and constant interest: to abandon the self-serving interests of slavery. It also motivates a love for the neighbor in difficulty, "for you were slaves in Egypt, and I delivered you." The church belongs to no nation, but is gathered from all. By faith in Christ living stones from all peoples form the temple of God, whose foundations go rock deep in the desert. Thus Paul enjoins complete separation from other temples and their deities: "Let us purify ourselves from everything that contaminates body and spirit, perfecting holiness out of reverence for God" (2 Cor. 7:1).

This purification takes place in the redemptively consecrated space of the body of Christ: the church-temple. There it is safe to speak of being loosed from the past and of struggling to wait

205

for the promised future, of fighting to move toward the new and away from the ever-nagging old. God's desert people is instructed but not yet competent; it complains and even rebels against the instruction of the Lord, it is immature as Paul's letters and church history demonstrate. During this transition the church struggles with her attraction to worldly culture (Ex. 16:3), suffers her incompetence and incompleteness. This constant testing of her loyalty is standard fare for Abraham's descendants (Gen. 22; James 1:1–4).

The time of separation and transition requires the discipline of self-denial: Denial of one's own past, culture, and ethnicity, as the soils that produce fruit worthy of repentance. Denial of worldly goods and interests as the land capable of sustaining this life without regard for the next. Denial of worldly power as the means to improve or even rescue the life of the neighbor caught up in the slavery to sin and its consequences. The time of separation and transition compels the church to be in but not of the world.

### The Desert Disciplines of Worship and Prayer

Neither God nor his people transform the desert. God transforms Abraham's descendants into slaves of righteousness within the space purified by his presence (Rom. 6:15–23). As oath-bound temple servants in the body of Christ, they scrupulously follow divine instruction to safeguard the church-temple's purity, to cleanse it when defiled, and to maintain its righteous order as a priestly community.

Central to the church-temple's identity is its communal worship. Organized to proclaim and praise God's mighty acts of salvation and sustenance, to lament the suffering caused by sin and sinners, to confess and plead for forgiveness of all that defiles, this gathering addresses the needs of the servants of righteousness on their way to the promised future.

Worship is fundamental for the church-temple for two reasons. First, life in the world daily challenges the oath-bound relationship with Christ. The world wants "just a little" room for unrighteousness, incites attraction to its pleasures and possibilities, and seeks to belittle the separation in Christ as insensitive, offensive to others, or merely superfluous. Second, life in the church-temple is permeated by temptations to forget what Christ has done, to hide from God, to blame him for life's problems, to regret the vow to worship him alone. The human heart above all is continually wicked, looking for its own way out of these predicaments (Gen. 6:5).

Oath-bound separation from the world and transition to newness of life require the discipline of communal worship and prayer. Without them oath-bound conduct languishes, for the church-temple's works of righteousness are but filthy rags (Isa. 64:6) whose efficacy will barely pass the fire of judgment (1 Cor. 3:11–15). Worship in God's presence reminds the church-temple of its true foundation; it sustains the church's life like nothing else can. Disciplined worship counters the world's priorities because in worship and through prayer God's people hear again and again what is most important about God and the world. They will be reaffirmed in the knowledge of who they truly are: not defiled by the world or their own hearts' deceptions, but purified by the consuming-fire presence of God through the Holy Spirit.

Although the church worships and prays in the world, the shape of the cult should not be determined by the world. Designed at Sinai for God's desert people, worship must remain clean of alien elements, for these defile the temple (2 Kings 21:1–18). Disciplined purification of the cult is the normal task

207

of the servants of righteousness in the church-temple (2 Kings 23:1–25; 1 Cor. 11:17–22); it prevents divine judgment, God's departure from his temple (Rev. 2–3; Ezek. 8–10), and his people's exile. In short, by covenant oath in God's presence, the church-temple vows to worship God in the world, but not by the world's standards; to pray for courage and strength to be servants of righteousness, not for the sake of the world, but for the sake of the purity of the body of Christ in the world. With such worship God's people will love him above all and their neighbor as themselves.

### The Desert Discipline of the Fear of the Lord

No more than her master does the church-temple have a place to lay her head. As a desert people she has no home, not even the Promised Land. All she has and needs is the promised presence and the canonical memory of what God has done and promises to do. These alone enable her to survive in the land as if it were the desert, and later in exile and in the Diaspora as if these were home.

The itinerary from Egypt through Sinai to Moab is fraught with fire. From the fire that raked Egypt in the seventh plague, to the pillar of cloud and fire which protected Israel from Egypt and from which the Lord attacked Egypt at the Sea, to the consuming fire of Sinai that moved into Israel's midst and consumed the burnt offerings to Israel's praise, and shortly thereafter, liturgically non-compliant Nadab and Abihu and the rebels at the edge of the camp. Israel experienced God both as good and as dangerous. The depicted journey teaches all generations of God's desert people how to live with that fire in their midst: close enough, as instructed, to receive illumination from it and live; not so close as to be consumed by it and die, nor so far from it as to be exiled into the desert's darkness. It is not the desert that gives or takes life.

This itinerary with the divine fire takes God's people from knowing the fear of Pharaoh to learning the fear of God (Ex. 14:10–13, 31); from the cunning to survive oppressive Egypt to a wisdom that brings forgiveness through sacrifice, cleanliness, and holiness through scrupulous attention to the words of life in the desert. Fearing this God means to trust and obey the words that came from Sinai's heights and subsequently from the divine dwelling place of the consuming fire. It is the nearness of this God and his words that are Israel's wisdom (Deut. 4:6–8). This they must teach their children (Deut. 31:12–13).

Torah craftiness sustains fear of the Lord and Israel's will to survive among the nations, whether in the Promised Land, in exile, or in the Diaspora (Esther; James 1:1). Awareness of God's consuming-fire presence at the center of oath-bound cult and conduct inculcates wisdom (Prov. 6:27–28), for the eyes of the Lord are upon the righteous and the wicked (Prov. 5:21–23), and all human plans are but fare for God's direction (Prov. 16:1–9).

Wisdom borne of the fear of the Lord distinguishes God's people from the nations who do not consider the heavenly Word a wisdom worth seeking (1 Cor. 1:18–2:4, esp. 1:26; James 3:13–18). In her desert journey, God's people learn the limitations of human wisdom, that one reaps what one sows, that people may propose but that God disposes, that "we" will not overcome (Gen. 11:5–9; Jer. 7:1–29) the world, and that we should not hide the light of God's presence under a bushel. There we also experience Folly's loud interruptions of Wisdom's steady invitation to fear the Lord (Prov. 9:1–6, 13–18). Living wisely in God's presence, God's people are always at home and on the way to their promised future.

## Conclusion: Living on the
## Land in This Present Age

The desert theology described above argues that this world is not the church's home, that she is waiting for the fullness of Christ's presence and the descent of the heavenly Jerusalem. Like the Jews of the book of Esther, the twelve tribes addressed by the apostle James who are scattered among the nations are far from home, but not without an identity and a vocation. Living in exile or the Diaspora is similar to living in the desert. It requires a sense of separation from the world and self-denial on the way to the promised future, an oath-bound cult and conduct, and a fear of the Lord that cultivates a torah wisdom for survival in this world—all with a lively sense of the presence of God through the Holy Spirit. These elements of a desert theology provide a realistic platform from which to address the issues of land ownership and management from the point of view of the divine presence.

First, the land promise is not about owning land, but about being owned and having been bought with a price. A tenant only manages another's land. In this time of waiting the only geography that truly matters to the church is the desert, and it reinforces separation from the world, self-denial, and total dependence on God. The desert is God's people's only inheritance; possession of the land remains in the future. Meanwhile, God's people, the church-temple, regularly seeks God's face in the cult to shape its conduct, and to hone its torah craftiness in the fear of the Lord, as required by the exigencies of the times in which the church exists.

Second, Judges, Kings, Jeremiah, and Ezekiel all show that God's people were terrible managers of the Promised Land, even when properly instructed and re-instructed by countless prophets who spoke to them from the very presence of God. The New Testament epistles and church history demonstrate that the body of Christ has not been a better manager of the entrusted gift of God's presence than was God's Old Testament people. Spiritual revivals have brought the church to a more disciplined practice of the desert theology now and then, but, "As a dog returns to its vomit, so a fool repeats his folly" (Prov. 26:11). There is little new under the sun.

Third, desert theology reminds the Church that it is the people in the desert who need transformation, not the desert itself. Indeed, Israel turned the land flowing with milk and honey into a wasteland filled with jackals, and God permitted enemies to salt the soil into enduring barrenness. Like the desert, land has no power of itself to give or sustain life. Only the water from a new temple will one day renew that land for good living (Ezek. 47:1–12; Rev. 22:1; Gen. 2:10–14; Ex. 15:22–27; 17:1–7), water that transforms all the sons and daughters of Adam and Eve into those who worship the only true God in spirit and in truth (John 4:13, 23–24).

Fourth, a desert theology does not encourage an other-worldly lifestyle, but another, distinct lifestyle in this world. It encourages a separation from sin and folly and a practice of righteousness and wisdom. Growth in wisdom and righteousness comes from meditation on God's Word (Josh. 1:8; Ps. 1:2) in communal worship, and a regular refocusing and reflection on God's presence and the Word that he speaks. Without these, daily conduct, including land management, will become corrupt and worldly.

How can life in God's presence solve the problems created by people movements from one land to another, land grabbing by squatters and empires, or the abuse of eminent domain laws for corporate or municipal benefit? None of these problems can

211

or will be solved until the Lord returns and scours this earth clean to people it with his own from all tribes and nations. And then even our best works will barely pass the test. For no human act of restoration or reparation can bring in a new world. While this present age endures, there will be wars, rumors of wars, suffering, pain, indebtedness, land grabbing, and ecological mismanagement. That is life in exile from the presence of God. Those whom God brings into his presence are not exempt from any of those abuses and their consequences, but by his grace they will experience and begin to practice—among themselves and with any neighbor God places on their way—what is righteous and wise in God's sight.

Emboldened by life in the presence of God, Christians will join with Jews, Palestinians, the people of Darfur, and the poor eking out a living in Cairo and Mexico City's garbage dumps to alleviate need and seek justice. Christians will not all have the same social or political point of view about these matters among themselves, for that is a matter of desert wisdom—"The first to present his case seems right, till another comes forward and questions him" (Prov. 18:17)—practiced out of fear of the Lord: "A king delights in a wise servant, but a shameful servant incurs his wrath" (Prov. 14:35; cf. 16:12–15). Wisdom needs prayer and centering worship, especially the opportunity to confess our folly before God and our neighbor. Thus we wait for the land.

# Index of Scripture

213

217

# Index of Subjects and Names